ACCLAIM FOR

Small Change

"Hay brings together in [*Small Change*] the revelatory power of narrative, the analytical possibilities of the personal essay and memoir, the investigative discipline of journalism, and the sudden illumination of lyric, and as a result she seems able to pick up almost everything – everything said, and most of what is only whispered in a gesture or a look between friends. . . . Endlessly rewarding. . . . These stories are beautifully written and carefully honed."

– The Malahat Review

"Stories that capture those details, moments, that someone less observant, less sensitive would miss. Language that flows as easily as water."

– Jury Citation, Governor General's Literary Awards

"Captivating. . . . Fluid, evanescent, rarely in balance, the friendships recounted in these stories are everything but peaceful." *– Toronto Star*

"Hay knows how to make a line breathe, and it's possible to open the book at random to find sharp, almost electric, prose leap out and give off light. . . . Through sparkling prose, Hay is able to flesh out the quirky and individual gestures that make out relationships. . . ."

– Ottawa X Press

"One of Canada's premier writers. . . ."

– Canadian Forum

BOOKS BY ELIZABETH HAY

FICTION

Crossing the Snow Line (stories, 1989)
Small Change (stories, 1997)
A Student of Weather (novel, 2000)

NON-FICTION

The Only Snow in Havana (1992)
Captivity Tales: Canadians in New York (1993)

Small Change

Elizabeth Hay

COUNTERPOINT
WASHINGTON, D.C.

First Counterpoint paperback edition 2001

McClelland & Stewart edition published 2000
First published by the Porcupine's Quill, Inc., 1997

Library of Congress Cataloging-in-Publication Data

     Hay, Elizabeth, 1951-
       Small change / Elizabeth Hay.
       p. cm.
       ISBN 1-58243-167-1 (pbk.: alk. paper)
        1. Women—Fiction.
        2. Female friendship—Fiction. I. Title.
       PR9199.3.H3676 S63 2001
       813'.54—dc21   2001028857

Some of the stories in this book first appeared in
The Capilano Review, *Quarry*, *Grain* and *Missing Jacket*.

The author is grateful to the Canada Council
for the Arts for its most generous support.

COUNTERPOINT
P.O. Box 65793
Washington, D.C. 20035-5793

Counterpoint is a member of the Perseus Books Group

10 9 8 7 6 5 4 3 2 1

This book is for my mother, my daughter,
and Sheila McCook

Her failure lay within herself, in her abrupt pride, and sudden sharp intolerance, and her inability, when in certain moods, to accept the small change of friendship, even from those who she knew loved her deeply.

Noël Coward, *Present Indicative*

You have to be clever to figure out how to be welcoming and defensive at the same time.

Toni Morrison, *Jazz*

CONTENTS

The Friend

She was thirty, a pale beautiful woman with long blond hair and high cheekbones, small eyes, sensuous mouth, an air of serenity and loftiness – superiority – and under that, nervousness, insecurity, disappointment. She was tired. There was the young child who woke several times a night. There was Danny who painted till two in the morning, then slid in beside her and coaxed her awake. There was her own passivity. She was always willing, even though she had to get up early, and always resentful, but never out loud. She complied. In conversation she was direct and Danny often took part, but in bed, apparently, she said nothing. She felt him slide against her, his hand between her legs, its motion the reverse of a woman wiping herself, back to front instead of front to back. She smelled paint – the air of the poorly ventilated attic where he worked – and felt his energetic weariness and responded with a weary energy of her own.

He didn't speak. He didn't call her by any name (during the day he called her Moe more often than Maureen). He reached across her and with practised efficiency found the Vaseline in the bedside drawer.

I met her one afternoon on the sidewalk outside the neighbourhood grocery store. It was sunny and it must have been warm – a Saturday in early June. Our section of New York was poor and Italian, and we looked very different from the dark women around us. The friendship began with that shorthand – shortcut to each other – an understanding that goes without saying. I had a small child too.

A week later, at her invitation, I walked the three blocks to her house and knocked on the front door. She opened a side door and called my name. "Beth," she said, "this way." She was dressed in a loose and colourful quilted top and linen pants. She looked composed and bohemian and from another class.

Inside there was very little furniture: a sofa, a chest, a rug, Danny's paintings on the wall. He was there. A small man with Fred Astaire's face and an ingratiating smile. Once he started to talk, she splashed into the conversation, commenting on everything he said and making it convoluted out of what I supposed was a desire to be included. Only later did I realize how much she insisted on being the centre of attention, and how successfully she became the centre of mine.

We used to take our kids to the only playground within walking distance. It was part of a school yard that marked the border between our neighbourhood and the next. The pavement shimmered with broken glass, the kids were wild and unattended. We pushed our two on the swings and kept each other company. She said she would be so mad if Danny got AIDS, and I thought about her choice of words – "so mad" – struck by the understatement.

I learned about sex from her the way girls learn about sex from each other. In this case the information came not in whispered conversations behind a hedge, but more directly and personally than anything I might have imagined at the age of twelve. In those days the hedge was high and green and the soil below it dark, a setting at once private, natural, and fenced off. This time everything was in the open. I was the audience, the friend with stroller, the mild-mannered wide-eyed listener who learned that breastfeeding brought her to the point of orgasm, that childbirth had made her vagina sloppy and loose, that anal sex hurt so much she would sit on the toilet afterwards, bracing herself against the stabs of pain.

We were in the playground (that sour, overused, wrongly used, hardly playful patch of pavement) and she said she was sore and told me why. When I protested on her behalf she said, "But I might have wanted it. I don't know. I think I did want it in some way."

I can't remember her hands, not here in this small cool room in another country and several years after the fact. I remember watching her do many things with her hands; yet I can't remember what they looked like. They must have been long, slender, pale unless tanned. But they don't come to mind the way a man's might and I suppose that's because she didn't touch me. Or is it because I became so adept at holding her at bay? I remember her lips, those dry thin Rock Hudson lips.

One evening we stood on the corner and she smiled her fleeting meaningful smiles, looking at me with what she called her northern eyes (they were blue and she cried easily) while her heartbreak of a husband put his arm around her. What will become of her, I wondered, even after I found out.

She was standing next to the stove and I saw her go up in flames: the open gas jets, the tininess of the room, the proximity of the children – standing on chairs by the stove – and her hair. It slid down her front and fell down her back. She was making pancakes that were obviously raw. She knew they were raw, predicted they would be, yet did nothing about it. Nor did I. I just poured on lots of syrup and said they were good.

I saw her go up in flames, or did I wish it?

In the beginning we saw each other almost every day and couldn't believe how much the friendship had improved our lives. A close, easy intensity which lasted in that phase of its life for several months. My husband talked of moving – an apartment had come open in a building where we had friends – but I couldn't imagine moving away from Maureen.

It was a throwback to girlhood, the sort of miracle that occurs when you find a friend with whom you can talk about everything.

Maureen had grown up rich and poor. Her family was poor, but she was gifted enough to receive scholarships to private schools. It was the private school look she had fixed on me the first time we met, and the poor background she offered later. As a child she received nothing but praise, she said, from parents astonished by their good fortune: They had produced a beautiful and brilliant daughter while everything else went wrong: car accidents, sudden deaths, mental illness.

Danny's private school adjoined hers. They met when they were twelve and he never tried to hide his various obsessions. She could never say that she had never known.

In the spring her mother came to visit. The street was torn up for repairs, the weather prematurely hot, the air thick with dust. Maureen had spread a green cloth over the table and set a vase of cherry blossoms in the middle. I remember the shade of green and the lushness of the blossoms because the sight was so out of character: everything about Maureen was usually in scattered disarray.

Her mother was tall, and more attractive in photographs than in person. In photographs she was still, in person she darted about, high-strung, high-pitched, erratic. Her rapid murmur left the same impression: startling in its abnormality, yet apparently normal. After years of endless talking about the same thing she now made the sounds that people heard: they had stopped up their ears long ago.

She talked about Maureen. How precocious she had been as a child, reading by the age of four and by the age of five memorizing whole books.

"I remember her reading a page, and I told her to go and read it to Daddy. She said, 'With or without the paper?' Lots of children can read at five, even her sister was reading at five, but few have Maureen's stamina. She could read for hours, and adult books. I had to put Taylor Caldwell on the top shelf."

A photograph of the child was tacked to the wall in Danny's studio. She was seated in a chair wearing one of those very short summer dresses we used to wear that ended well above bare round knees. Her face was unforgettable. It was more than beautiful. It had a direct, knowing, almost luminous look produced by astonishingly clear eyes and fair, fair skin. Already she knew enough not to smile.

"That's her," said Danny. "There she is."

The beautiful kernel of the beautiful woman.

She had always imagined bodies firmer than hers but not substantially different. She had always imagined Danny with a boy.

I met the lover without realizing it. It was late summer, we were at their house in the country, a shaded house beside a stream – cool, green, quiet – the physical manifestation of the serenity I once thought she possessed. A phrase in a movie review: her wealth so old it had a patina. Maureen's tension so polished it had a fine sheen.

All weekend I picked her long hairs off my daughter's sweater and off my own. I picked them off the sheet on the bed. I picked blackberries, which left hair-like scratches on my hands.

My hands felt like hers. I looked down at my stained fingers and they seemed longer. I felt the places where her hands had been, changing diapers, buttoning shirts, deep in tofu and tahini, closing in on frogs which she caught with gusto. Swimming, no matter how cold.

I washed my hands and lost that feeling of being in contact with many things. Yet the landscape continued – the scratches if not the smells, the sight of her hands and hair.

An old painter came to visit. He parked his station wagon next to the house and followed Danny into his studio in the barn. Maureen and I went off with the kids to pick berries. It was hot and humid. There would be rain in the night and again in the morning. We followed a path through the woods to a stream where the kids splashed about while Maureen and I dangled our feet over the bank. Her feet were long and slender, mine were wide and short. We sent ripples of water towards the kids.

She told me that Henry – the painter's name was Henry – was Danny's mentor, they had known each other for years and he was a terrible alcoholic. Then she leaned so close her shoulder touched mine. One night last summer Danny had come back from Henry's studio and confessed – confided – that he had let the old man blow him. Can you believe it? And she laughed – giddy – flushed – excited – and eager, it seemed, to impress me with her sexual openness and to console herself with the thought that she had impressed me. A warm breeze blew a strand of her hair into my face. I brushed it away and it came back – ticklish, intimate, warm and animal-like. I didn't find it unpleasant, not at the time.

We brought the berries back to the house, and late in the afternoon the two men emerged to sit with us on the verandah. Henry was whiskery, gallant, shy. Maureen talked a great deal and laughed even more. Before dark, Henry drove away.

She knew. It all came out the next spring and she pretended to be horrified, but she knew.

That night sounds woke me: Danny's low murmur, Maureen's uninhibited cries. I listened for a long time. It must have occurred to me then that the more gay he was, the more she was aroused.

I thought it was someone come to visit. But the second time I realized it was ice falling. At midday, icicles fall from the eavestrough into the deep snow below.

And the floor which I keep sweeping for crumbs? There are no crumbs. The sound comes from the old linoleum itself. It crackles in the cold.

Often I wake at one or two in the morning, overheated from the hot water bottle, the three blankets, the open sleeping bag spread on top. In my dreams I take an exam over and over again.

In the morning I go down in the socks I've worn all night to turn up the heat and raise the thin bamboo blind through which everyone can see us anyway. I make coffee, then scald milk in a hand-beaten copper pot with a long handle. Quebec has an expression for beating up egg whites: *monter en neige*. Milk foams up and snow rises.

Under the old linoleum old newspapers advertise an "equipped one bedroom at Lorne near Albert" for $175. Beside the porch door the linoleum has broken away and you can read mildew, dust, grit, *Ottawa Citizen*, May 1, 1979. The floor is a pattern of squares inset with triangles and curlicues in wheat shades of immature to ripe. Upstairs the colours are similar but faded; and flowers, petals.

During the eclipse last month I saw Maureen when I saw the moon. I saw my thumb inch across her pale white face.

I have no regrets about this. But I have many thoughts.

We pushed swings in the playground while late afternoon light licked at the broken glass on the pavement. New York's dangers were all around us, as was Maureen's fake laugh. She pushed William high in the swing, then let out a little trill each time he came swooping back.

It was the time of Hedda Nussbaum. We cut out the stories in the newspaper and passed them back and forth – photographs of Hedda's beaten face, robust husband, abused and dead daughter. It had been going on for so long. Hedda had been beaten for thirteen years, the child was seven years old.

In the playground, light licked at the broken glass and then the light died and we headed home. Often we stopped for tea at Maureen's. Her house always had a loose and welcoming atmosphere which hid the sharp edge of need against which I rubbed.

She began to call before breakfast, dressing me with her voice, her worries, her anger, her malleability. Usually she was angry with Danny for staying up so late that he was useless all day, of no help in looking after William, while she continued to work to support them, to look after the little boy in the morning and evening, to have no time for herself. But when I expressed anger on her behalf she defended him . . .

Similarly with the stomach pains. An ulcer, she suggested, then made light of the possibility when I took it seriously.

She would ask, "Is this all? Is this going to be my contribution?" She was referring to her brilliant past and her sorry present: her pedestrian job, the poor neighbourhood, her high-maintenance husband when there were any number of men she could have married, any number she said. Motherhood gave her something to excel at. She did everything for her son – dressed him, fed him, directed every moment of play. "Is this all right, sweetie? Is this? What about this? Then, sweetie pie, what do you want?"

Sweetie pie wanted what he got. His mother all to himself for a passionately abusive hour, then peace, affection. During a tantrum she would hold him in her lap behind a closed door, then emerge half an hour later with a small smile. "That was a short one. You should see what they're like sometimes."

Even when Danny offered to look after him, even when he urged her to take a long walk, she refused. Walked, but briefly, back and forth on the same sidewalk, or up and down the same driveway. Then returned out of a sense of responsibility to the child. But the child was fine.

At two years he still nursed four or five times a night and her nipples were covered with scabs. "But the skin there heals so quickly," she said.

We moved to the other side of the city and the full force of it hit me. I remember bending down under the sink of our new apartment, still swallowing a mouthful of peanut butter, to cram S.O.S pads into the hole – against the mouse, taste of it, peanut butter in the trap. Feel of it, dry and coarse under my fingers. Look of it, out of the corner of my eye a small dark slipper. Her hair always in her face, and the way I was ratting on her.

It got to the point where I knew the phone was going to ring before it rang. Instead of answering, I stood there counting. Thirty rings. Forty. Once I told her I thought she had called earlier, I was in the bathroom and the phone rang forever. Oh, she said, I'm sorry, I wasn't even paying attention. Then I saw the two of us: Maureen mesmerized by the act of picking up a phone and holding it for a time; and me, frantic with resentment at being swallowed whole.

"Why is she so exhausting?" I asked my husband. Then answered my own question. "She never stops talking and she always talks about the same thing."

But I wasn't satisfied with my answer. "She doesn't want solutions to her problems. That's what is so exhausting."

And yet that old wish – a real wish – to get along. I went to bed thinking about her, woke up thinking about her and something different, yet related, the two mixed together in a single emotion. I had taken my daughter to play with her friend Joyce, another girl was already there and they didn't want Annie to join them. I woke up thinking of my daughter's rejection, my own various rejections, and Maureen.

It seemed inevitable that he would leave her – clear that he was gay and therefore inevitable that he would leave her. He was an artist. To further his art he would pursue his sexuality.

But I was wrong; he didn't leave her. And neither did I.

Every six months he had another gay attack and talked, thought, drew penises. Every six months she reacted predictably and never tired of her reactions, her persistence taking on huge, saintly proportions. As for me, I never initiated a visit or a call, but I didn't make a break. As yielding as she was, and she seemed to be all give, Danny and I were even more so.

Tensions accumulated – the panic as she continued to call and I continued to come when called, though each visit became more abrasive, more insulting, as though staged to show who cared least: You haven't called me, you never call me, you think you can make up for your inattention with this visit but I'll show you that I don't care either: the only reason I'm here is so that my son can play with your daughter.

We walked along the river near her country place. William was on the good tricycle, my daughter on the one that didn't work. Maureen said, "I don't think children should be forced to share. Do you? I think kids should share when they want to share."

Her son would not give my daughter a turn the whole long two-hour walk beside the river – with me pointing out what? Honeysuckle. Yes, honeysuckle. Swathes of it among the rocks. And fishermen with strings of perch. I stared out over the river, unable to look at Maureen and not arguing; I couldn't find the words.

With each visit there was the memory of an earlier intimacy, and no interest in resurrecting it. Better than nothing. Better than too much. And so it continued, until it spun lower.

We were sitting on the mattress on the floor of Danny's studio in front of a wall-sized mirror. Around us were his small successful paintings and his huge failures. He insisted on painting big, she said, because he was so small. "I really think so. It's just machismo."

How clear-eyed she was.

I rested my back against the mirror, Maureen faced it. She glanced at me, then the mirror, and each time she looked in the mirror she smiled slightly. Her son was there. He wandered off and then it became clear that she was watching herself.

She told me she was pregnant again. It took two years to persuade Danny, "and now he's even more eager than I am," smiling at herself in the mirror.

Danny got sick. I suppose he had been sick for months, but I heard about it in the spring. Maureen called in tears. "The shoe has dropped," she said.

He was so sick that he had confessed to the doctors that he and Henry – old dissipated Henry whose cock had slipped into who knows what – had been screwing for the last five years. Maureen talked and wept for thirty minutes before I realized that she had no intention of leaving him, or he of leaving her. They would go on. The only change, and this wasn't certain, was that they wouldn't sleep together. They would go to their country place in June and stay all summer.

I felt cheated, set up, used. "Look, you should *do* something," I said. "Make some change."

She said, "I know. But I don't want to precipitate any-thing. Now isn't the time."

She said it wasn't AIDS.

Her lips dried out like tangerine sections separated in the morning and left out all day. She nursed her children so long that her breasts turned into small apricots, and now I cannot hold an apricot in my hand and feel its soft loose skin, its soft non-weight, without thinking of small spent breasts – little dugs.

She caught hold of me, a silk scarf against an uneven wall, and clung.

Two years later I snuck away. In the weeks leading up to the move, I thought I might write to her afterwards, but in the days immediately before, I knew I would not. One night in late August when the weather was cool and the evenings still long, we finished packing at nine and pulled away in the dark.

We turned right on Broadway and rode the traffic in dark slow motion out of the city, north along the Hudson, and home.

In Canada I thought about old friends who were new friends because I hadn't seen them for such a long time. And newer friends who were old friends because I'd left them behind in the other place. And what I noticed was that I had no landscape in which to set them. They were portraits in my mind (not satisfying portraits either, because I couldn't remember parts of their bodies; their hands, for instance, wouldn't come to mind). They were emotion and episode divorced from time and place. Yet there was a time – the recent past, and a place – a big city across the border.

And here was I, where I had wanted to be for as long as I had been away from it – home – and it didn't register either. In other words, I discovered that I wasn't in a place. I was the place. I felt populated by old friends. They lived in my head amid my various broodings. Here they met again, going through the same motions and different ones. Here they coupled in ways that hadn't occurred really. And here was I, disloyal but faithful, occupied by people I didn't want to see and didn't want to lose.

September came and went, October came and went, winter didn't come. It rained in November, it rained again in December. In January a little snow fell, then more rain.

Winter came when I was asleep. One morning I looked out at frozen puddles dusted with snow. It was very cold. I stepped carefully into the street and this is what I saw. I saw the landscape of friendship. I saw Sunday at four in the afternoon. I saw childhood panic. People looked familiar to me, yet they didn't say hello. I saw two people I hadn't seen in fifteen years, one seated in a restaurant, the other skating by. I looked at them keenly, waiting for recognition to burst upon them, but it didn't.

Strangers claimed to recognize me. They said they had seen me before, some said precisely where. "It was at a conference two years ago." Or, "I saw you walk by every day with your husband last summer. You were walking quickly."

But last summer Ted and I had been somewhere else.

The connections were wistful, intangible, maddening. Memory tantalized before it finally failed. Yet as much as memory failed, those odd, unhinged conjunctures helped. Strange glimmerings and intense looks were better than nothing.

The last time I saw Maureen, she was wearing a black-and-white summer dress and her teeth were chattering. "Look at me," she said, her mouth barely able to form the words, her lower jaw shaking. "It's not that cold."

We were in the old neighbourhood. The street was dark and narrow with shops on either side, and many people. I was asking my usual questions, she was doing her best to answer them.

"Look," she said again, pointing to her lips which were shaking uncontrollably.

I nodded, drew my jacket tight, mentioned how much warmer it had been on the way to the café, my voice friendly enough but without the intonations of affection and interest, the rhythms of sympathy, the animation of friendship. In the subway we felt warm again. She waited for my train to come, trying to redeem and at the same time distance herself. I asked about Danny and she answered. She talked about his job, her job, how little time each of them had for themselves. She went on and on. Before she finished I asked about her children. Again she talked.

"I don't mean to brag," she said, helpless against the desire to brag, "but Victoria is so verbal."

Doing to her children and for herself what her mother had done to her and for herself.

"So verbal, so precocious. I don't say this to everyone," listing the words that Victoria already knew.

She still shivered occasionally. She must have known why I didn't call any more, aware of the reasons while inventing others in a self-defence that was both pathetic and dignified. She never asked what went wrong. Never begged for explanations (dignified even in her begging: her persistence as she continued to call and extend invitations).

We stood in the subway station – one in a black-and-white dress, the other in a warm jacket – one hurt and pale, the other triumphant in the indifference which had taken so long to acquire. We appeared to be friends. But a close observer would have seen how static we were, rooted in a determination not to have a scene, not to allow the other to cause hurt. Standing, waiting for my train to come in.

The Fire

I t's late. When snow falls at night this room is lighter because falling snow brightens the streetlight and again afterwards because the moon comes out and shines on the new snow. Movie sets use Styrofoam panels to extend the day. The same principle applies: a pulsing between two sources of brightness: snow and moon, Styrofoam and sun, night-shirt and frypan. I learned about the fire in a letter from Maureen's older sister Jill.

"We started out at opposite points," Jill said to me once when we were talking about Maureen, "and now we've come together." She meant that my liking had turned to dislike and her dislike had softened.

Behind her glasses Jill's eyes were tentative and on hold. She was the one who seemed to know so little, yet knew everything. She knew about Danny's affair with Henry and his various flirtations, and she predicted how everything would end. What she predicted unfolded before her eyes.

One Sunday morning in June she was drinking coffee while reading a book in a small café in the Village. Jill was always reading, a professional disease, she said, it goes with being a librarian. Her visits to the Village were to see her two troubled sons and her various doctors. For as long as I knew her, she was solicitous, stoical, and ill.

Her table was beside a row of windows overlooking the street. For a moment she looked up, her eyes shifting past parking meters and cars, and saw Danny. He was at the corner with his arm around a pretty young woman. The light turned, they crossed the street and walked right past her window without seeing her.

She had to smile. Danny had done the unpredictable by doing the most predictable thing of all. She said to me, "I felt the way a novelist must feel when her characters come to life."

Danny's sweet young thing, as Jill called her, was a student painter who had gone to him for advice. Maureen reacted (I swear this is true) by taking up painting.

❖

She gets up early while the others sleep, makes chamomile tea and drinks it with honey, then sits down at her work table beside the window. This is easier to imagine than what she paints. I suspect she paints picture after picture of the same empty bed.

Her skin absorbs paint. She takes to it as a dry wall, untouched for years, soaks up gallon after gallon of colour. Or a city in decline surrenders to the paintbrush and then the fire. Her hands go yellow, green, blue – a rainbow bruise extending up her wrists.

One afternoon she puts away freshly washed laundry and notices drops of blood on the white sheets. She looks at her palms and sees on her fingers splits as fine as paper cuts. This hasn't happened since she was a child. In those days she refused salves and creams, so every night her mother waited until she had fallen asleep, then snuck into her room and rubbed her hands with oil and her lips with Vaseline. Under her mother's shiny fingertip, Maureen's chapped lips moved like relaxed limbs. That was the first of the nightly Vaseline rituals.

Let's say it's two in the morning. Let's say the window is open and light from the street falls on the bed. Danny undresses. His face is all bone – teeth, nose, high forehead – but his body is shapely. Maureen has told me how fine his legs are, how fine his chest. His cock waves a little – uncertain top-heavy bloom – smooth and shiny tulip past its prime. Women scrub floors until their hands are the same colour and equally shiny.

Her panic is almost permanent now. She is awake, she wants to talk, but he hushes her. She has the children, which she wanted; they are together still and she wants that. He lies down beside her. Again she tries to talk. "I have no friends. No one ever calls –"

"Shhhh."

The only man in her life. The only man who has known her since girlhood and has witnessed her in her glory. The panic: not that there is nothing she can do (she works, she earns, she raises children), but that there is nothing she can do well. A form of amnesia has taken over and she cannot remember how it was that she ever excelled.

She goes into Danny's studio. She often goes in to look at his work and to see what he has in the small fridge in the corner. This time his notebook is lying on top of the fridge. In her hands it falls open to a male nude asleep in a manner that affords no rest. She thinks of an udder unmilked for days, something unbearably heavy, and feels simultaneously aroused and sad. Even in sleep he has to lug this thing around. The drawing could be a Biblical representation of Lust. It is a good drawing too.

In some ways they are closer than ever. Even more than before, he confides his artistic ambitions and sexual doubts. She listens. She sits on the pale yellow sofa in their barely furnished living room and keeps track. Sometimes her mind wanders, sometimes she turns away in fatigue, but in general she keeps track.

"You're my best friend," he says, and it would have consoled her once. Victoria is two, William is five. "I can tell you anything."

Here she is, a woman who has tormented and aroused herself with the thought of young boys in her husband's bed, and what lovers does he take? An old sadsack of a drunk and a young woman. Where does that leave her?

"Where does that leave me?" she asks.

She sees him disappearing, yet her footsteps are the ones filling with sand, hers are the fingerprints vanishing off the wall. He will nęver leave the house, he will never leave his studio.

By the end of the summer she no longer wants to keep abreast of his every thought and she wants to tell someone in exactly those words. *I no longer want to keep abreast.* But no one calls.

She runs her hand along the back of the sofa, releasing old dust into the late afternoon light. She looks beyond the stirred and shining air, beyond the disturbances in her life (dusty beautiful spore-filled air; a potential for flowers) to the phone.

She doesn't remember, except intuitively, the nightly occurrence of fingers smoothing her lips, stroking the skin under her nose and the edges of her nostrils, but when her mother returns to apply ointments, she finds that she already knows about this comfort, has acquired the knowledge the way you learn a language by listening to a tape while you sleep. Her mother returns in September after the fire.

Maureen had risen early with the kids. She hadn't bothered to change out of her long cotton T-shirt and was still wearing it at noon. Victoria was napping, the boy was playing in the living room. He was hungry.

Maureen went into the kitchen to make pancakes. Sun poured into the kitchen while she poured oil into an aluminum frypan. The oil shone, the pan shone, her white T-shirt shone. And because she was leaning into the stove, because she was so close to the gas jet, because the white of her shirt fed the hot white light of the pan and the light of the pan bounced back to her shirt and back to the pan and back to her shirt, and perhaps because grease spat onto her shirt, (no one ever fully understood), it caught fire.

Danny was in the bath. He always had a bath when he got up around noon. Sometimes he locked the door, sometimes he wore a Walkman. It depended on his mood. There was another bathroom in the basement, if Maureen or the kids needed to pee they went there. He liked the bath to be full and hot, and the music loud.

Maureen sprang away from the stove and flames shot up to her face. There was a sink right there. She knew there was a sink, she knew she needed water. Nevertheless, she fled the kitchen. Later she would say that she wanted to get as far away as possible from the stove, it was only natural.

She ran screaming into the living room. But Danny didn't hear.

She tore a piece of fabric off the wall, an old, dry, embroidered piece of fabric from Peru. She slapped it against her chest and it went up like kindling.

She banged on the bathroom door and still he didn't hear. He didn't hear her, or the fire alarm, or the boy's screams.

And so she ran at the door. She backed up (this would be the lasting image in the boy's head: his mother on fire charging a locked door) and ran at it with her shoulder, knocking it halfway off its hinges and somersaulting into the bathtub.

My old neighbours heard the ambulance. Laura heard it on her way home from the hairdresser's and told Clara. "She was

wearing this sheet and he had his arm around her, and I says
to myself, I says, what happened to the baby?"

It was half past noon on a Friday. There wasn't a cloud in
the sky.

❖

We used to sit outside in the evening, Laura, Clara, Cathy
and I, under the shadow of Frank. We would hear the sound
of the second-floor window being raised behind us, and
stiffen. I never looked up. Laura looked up.

"It's your husband," she would say to Cathy. And our talk
would die on our lips.

We stayed out there till early September in a long slow
slide from bare arms to sweaters to jackets, as the streetlights
came on earlier and earlier and the air cooled down. Frank
would come out with his pursed lips and barely perceptible
nod, his slicked-back arrogant looks, and stand on *his* stoop
whose outer sidewalk we, as tenants, could use. He would
walk down the street saving his jocularity for certain men and
his smiles for certain young women.

Last night I dreamt about Frank. We laughed together.
He was sitting across the table and reached for my bag
of tortilla chips. I nodded, then poked him in the chest.
"Now you owe me one," I said. He laughed, or at least he
smiled. How strange that dreams can make such friendliness possible.

The poinsettia has died but I haven't pitched it yet. It sits
on the table next to the wide window that overlooks the playground (Canadian and glass-free) and the complicated and

expensive play structure that dominates it. A memorial to simple childhood. May it rest.

Laura's words whenever she referred to her daughter. "I fed my daughter – may she rest – puddings and cakes and candy all the time. Never did no harm," and she emptied her pockets of sweets into my daughter's eager hands. Laura's daughter died in a diabetic coma at the age of forty-two.

I tiptoed up the stairs to avoid Laura for one reason and Frank for another. To avoid the punishing excesses of Laura's company (the mountains of macaroni and gravy she forced upon me) and to avoid any contact with Frank, of whom I had an unreasoning dread. But why unreasoning? It's too bad I was so afraid of him, but it wasn't unreasonable. I have never had Ted's capacity – as natural and pervasive as dew – to ignore people.

We were sitting in Laura's kitchen. Laura and I were at the kitchen table, Clara was in the rocking chair talking about her second pregnancy forty years ago. She craved apples, she said. In those days an apple tree grew in Laura's backyard, but Clara was new to the country, and shy, and didn't ask. As time went on and she continued to forgo the apple, she became convinced the baby would be "marked" in some way. She gave birth and to her horror the baby's face – as babies' faces often are – was streaked with red. She thought it was the apple.

Eat everything you crave, said Laura. If you don't, the baby will get marks.

Yes, she said. My aunt had this longing for wine and she always sat like this (she rested her cheek in the palm of her hand), and my niece was born with a wine hand on her face.

I was wearing one of Maureen's pregnancy dresses – a pink sundress with three small buttons at the back, the top one of which kept catching my hair, pulling my head gradually back and reminding me of the Ferris wheel. She was seventeen when it happened. After they extricated her – cutting away long blond hair wound so tightly around the cable that her head arched back – she had a bald spot the size of a fifty-cent piece.

In her dresses I wore her. Or she wore me? Which? She was covering my body, but I was inside her dress. People confused us with each other. One morning the newspaper vendor gave me a message about a possible babysitter, thinking he was giving a message to her.

Another morning I showered, then reached into the closet for one of her dresses. The right sleeve had come loose. I got out needle and thread and spent ten minutes mending it. The dress was mauve and white, striped and long. While I mended I read a story in the paper about a woman who had carried her sewing into the living room, her needle in one hand, what she was sewing in the other, and accidentally knocked against the doorway and driven the needle into her heart.

I miscarried that afternoon, and two months later Maureen was telling me she was pregnant.

❖

There is a process in friendship of becoming the other person, and of erasing yourself and the other person in the process. You see the friend turn away, and in that moment you stop seeing the friend and see only yourself as someone turned away from.

I was never able to keep all of her in my mind at once, the person I had liked and the person I came to dislike. I remember standing beside her in the Korean fruit store while she bent down to smell a hyacinth in a pot, her long unwashed hair swinging into her face and mingling with the other smell – one sweet and otherworldly, the other salty and human. The smell of spring and the smell of panic.

Whenever her son whimpered in the night, she left Danny's side and lay down beside him till morning. She slept poorly because of the narrow bed and because of dreams in which young men appeared, intent on following her and eager to make love. She would wake in tears at the contrast between what she might have had, and what she had.

Her mother cornered me in the playground. Another visit, almost the same time of year: April, and the wind kept blowing her words away. She couldn't understand why Maureen's talents had borne so little fruit. If only she had more time. "She is *so* jealous," she said, "of the time you have to write."

In that moment I felt a cool wind of ill will blow against my skin – just enough to open up my own storehouse of negativity. I remembered the Russian tale I had read with such a sense of recognition. A peasant was given the chance to choose anything he wanted so long as his neighbour got twice as much. He thought and thought, and finally chose to have one of his eyes put out.

What was the word Maureen used as we went upstairs, the German word for joy at another's sorrow?

"I don't mean that," she said. "Not that dramatic. But, yes, I'm jealous of anybody's time, especially my husband's," and she laughed.

We were halfway up the stairs, she turned around to speak to me, and there was a small smile on her face. The Germans have a word for it.

I walked back home and looked out the window at Clara's garden next door. It was one of the most beautiful gardens I had ever seen. A narrow sidewalk, two steps, and where the steps rose, a low, roughly made stone wall. Beyond the wall under the magnolia small stones separated semi-circles of ground. It was a poor, graceful, hardworking garden that would produce abundantly all summer long. I opened the window and in surged the smell of laundry soap from down the street. A last snow flurry, a late spring.

A day later it surprised me how much her comments still bothered me. Bothered me more as I didn't hear from her, as I deliberately left the house early and unplugged the phone when I came home, so that I couldn't hear from her. Then walked down the block looking for her in the distance.

❖

What saved her was the lanolin she always rubbed into her nipples after nursing the children. She made a habit of spreading it around her chest and in the end it protected her skin from the fire. Jill wrote that she healed very quickly. In a few months she was probably an older version of the wedding snapshot taken when they were twenty-two. Danny and a friend of his had their arms around her thin shoulders,

she was looking down at the ground, she was smiling (unlike
the child who knew enough not to smile), and her hair was
cropped close to her head. It formed a soft helmet, and yes,
she looked like a boy.

Cézanne in a Soft Hat

Soon after we moved here, I picked up a small book about Cézanne. This was in September. I opened the book to dry landscapes and cool still lifes, to late summer and early fall, to the pleasure and pain of seasonal change, the detachment of weather. This is the detachment we seek and usually fail to find in friendships – an unbegrudging, clear-eyed, undemanding, infinitely interesting and natural presence.

Here were pears on a table, apples in a bowl, a flowered pitcher, a leafy piece of fabric. Everything gave the impression of being aware of every other thing but in a way that transcends the human.

I began to read the biographical notes and came upon the description of Cézanne's friendship with Zola, a deep and long friendship that began in Aix in 1852 when Cézanne was thirteen, and ended in 1886 when Zola published a novel about a painter who hanged himself in front of the painting he couldn't complete. Everyone knew the painter was Cézanne.

I reread the paragraph about the end of their friendship. "Although he spoke of it to no one, it could be seen that Cézanne's grief was bitter and irremediable. Perhaps it was partly because of the sincere compassion expressed in the novel that Cézanne's grief was so inconsolable."

I wondered how sincere Zola's compassion was. I wondered how it was known that Cézanne's grief was inconsolable if he spoke of it to no one, and how it was known that he spoke of it to no one. I wondered about Zola's ulterior motives – his desire to hurt an old friend, his competitiveness, his honesty, his dishonesty. The book said that Zola had moved away from his Impressionist friends and no longer believed in them, having been their most valiant champion. But my main interest was Cézanne and the way he dealt with the discovery that his oldest and dearest friend considered him a failure and used him as subject matter in a book.

No more letters passed between them, apparently. There were no more greetings, and they did not meet again.

In 1886 Cézanne was forty-seven. His friendship with Zola had lasted more than thirty years. The first time Zola left for Paris and Cézanne remained in Aix, they were about twenty. Cézanne wrote to him: "Ever since you left I am tormented by grief. This is the truth. You would not recognize me. I feel heavy, stupid and slow."

The book has two self-portraits: an unfinished sketch in 1880 when he was forty-one, half bald, heavy forehead, dark beard, large face; then *Cézanne in a Soft Hat* ten years later, several years after the break with Zola and several years in the making. His nose and chin are more pointed than broad; his beard is white and grey; the colours of his coat, hat, and jacket are repeated in the colours of the wall; and he seems less massive – flimsier and more decorative. He is known for his persistence in the face of doubts and for how slowly he painted.

In early October we were beside a river with two friends. The woman was telling us that old friends of theirs had just moved away. They had moved away one morning, and in the afternoon she had walked past the empty house and couldn't believe how relieved she felt. She laughed about it and went on talking, compelled to tell us, her new friends, about these old friends.

She said it was the woman in the couple who had pulled away, and she had never understood why. Simply, the invitations stopped, the Christmas gifts ended, various courtesies vanished. With their disappearance arrived her confusion and sense of hurt, so that when she walked her dog past their house she was never sure whether the woman came down the steps because she wanted to say hello, or because she felt she had to.

She said, "I talked a lot about work with him, maybe she felt left out. And then she went through a lot of changes herself and got her own friends."

But none of these reasons was sufficient to explain a change so drastic, and she knew it.

She peeled a peach as she told the story. She avoided the words *dropped* or *dumped* or *rejected*. She said only that she didn't understand, that once there had been steady contact and then there was none, that whenever they saw each other they all enjoyed themselves, but afterwards there was nothing.

The peach was from the market, carried in a knapsack, a little bruised and one of eight. She peeled another, her fingers curving around the fruit, picking at the peel with her fingernail, then pulling it back. We sat on a blanket on the grass and ate tomatoes, bread, cheese, the peaches, a sausage. We ate with our hands and shared a napkin.

My friend dealt with being rejected by understanding and not understanding, stating and understating, avoiding certain things but staying true to the general picture. Her husband was impatient. He couldn't be bothered, he said, worrying about such things.

This is the refreshing thing about men. They don't brood so luxuriously about friendships gone wrong. They think about them very little, it seems, and talk about them less. Cézanne, for instance.

Ted said, "It's hard when one person wants the friendship and another doesn't. People change."

But that only rubbed salt in the wound. Our friend wasn't saying they didn't want her, she was saying they seemed to enjoy her company and this was the source of her confusion. She was unable to give up the hope that she was liked.

I was thinking about her again this morning when I peeled a peach. I used the fingers of my left hand, picking the skin loose at the top as you pick one page free from the page below.

I was thinking about a conversation with Maureen. We were in a park and it was warm, it might have been late spring or early fall. We were sitting on a stone wall and she was distributing food to the kids. (She was always much more prepared than I, never leaving the house without a variety of snacks and drinks.) She could not believe, she said, that certain friends with whom she had been incredibly close had faded away – she mentioned a roommate in university – yet she admitted it was so with tight lips, and I knew she foresaw our own end.

My sympathies are with Cézanne even though I am like Zola – the realistic writer using the people he knows. What defence can Zola offer? When accused of using the life of a friend to further his artful ends, what can he say? That it was his life too? It was my life too.

The Kiss

My children are asleep in the car. The last of the sun comes over the trees and falls on the porch where I sit. Maybe it's the sight of the car with kids inside or my thoughts about Johnny, but I remember and dwell upon an early moment of almost exalted excitement. I was five, a child on the lawn waiting for a friend to arrive. The lawn was rough, poorly tended, and the house ramshackle. Its front porch concealed a treasure trove of lost objects under the steps: lipsticks in brass tubes, combs, broken bits of crockery half embedded in damp soil. I would be on my knees in that dark little place reaching through the horror of spider webs on my wrists for something shiny. A strip of grass separated the porch from the driveway. I waited there. Every so often I ran inside to look at the clock and to ask my mother the time, aching at the delay.

What happened between then and now? Between the child who felt nothing but delight at the prospect of seeing an old friend, and the woman who cannot bear to be visited?

Sound of tires on gravel, illumination of leaves long before the headlights appear. People are arriving home from the city, they leave early and arrive now.

This is Johnny and Lee's house, and I am here while they are away.

When I was a child, my father used to stare off into space while his lips moved and his fingers worked a napkin. He preferred to communicate with the stone walls he made and the flowers he grew. In his dressing gown and with boyish eagerness, he would clip several lilies, put them in a vase and bring them to the breakfast table.

I usually describe my father as a man given to impenetrable solitude. If I turn the phrase I can apply it to Johnny. Impenetrable happiness. For a long time I couldn't enter his life because his happiness, or appearance of happiness – his unending smiles – locked the door. An ingenious strategy, to surround the thorns with a castle.

But now I have penetrated. I am in the castle.

I pause to touch things with that combination of curiosity, affection, and ill will that characterizes adult friendships. I touch bottles of perfume, open them, smell them, dab my wrists, and for a few minutes become Lee. I smell the way she does and hear the same sounds, wake at the same hour on the same pillow in the same light. I have a right to be here because I am a friend, and so my intrusion is even stealthier, even more complete.

"You were much nicer to her than she was to you," my mother said about the little friend who came by car. "You were very generous. I had to interfere because you gave her all your dolls."

How do you get from there to here? From the unsuspicious longing for a friend, the generous early regard, the pure happiness in her company (a little awkwardness in the first moments, my friend tired from the drive, but soon we were playing in every room of the house) to here. The occupation of a friend's house, and the wilful eagerness to find fault.

The first time I saw Johnny he was leaning against a car, smoking a cigarette and lost in thought. A month later we were on the beach together with a group of friends. It was late afternoon, we were stretched out on towels, and I said it almost in passing. "I have good news."

His look was immediate, instinctive, unguarded. The look of someone facing an unexpected trespasser, a look of open and hostile reevaluation. I saw him register the news, I saw his view of me shift, and his resistance to the shift.

Once his face returned to normal he told me about his own plans, something he had never bothered to do and which he now did in great detail. He didn't seem to care that he was underscoring how little I had registered, how easily and happily he had dismissed me.

I saw that look in his eyes a few more times. It didn't have the nakedness of the first occasion but I recognized it: a deliberate erasure of expression. I wondered what had started it. His envy or mine.

He left instructions about what to do with his garden. For two days I prune the forsythia, the mock orange, the lilac. The kids drag the clippings off to one side and make a hut. They tucker themselves out and at five o'clock the youngest falls asleep. I hold his small hand, feel the fibrillations, trepidations, movements of a small animal in sleep.

At night I close my eyes and down come forsythia leaves like soft green blotting paper. Even later, when I return to the city and cars pass by on the treeless street, these leafy forms swim into my mind.

❖

You meet someone and take on their hue, form, tone, but against your will. They sleep in the next room and you can't sleep. They are intruders who steal you away and leave you nothing for yourself.

You feel observed, not by the friend but by his presence. It's as though you are being photographed in the dark. Nothing of you comes out, but the photographer is large and clear.

❖

It was nighttime. We were coming back from a walk through the woods, moving past the cars in the driveway towards the porch light, when Johnny spoke about his family. Their first instinct was never the generous one, he said, and

neither was his. He was going to try to make it so. He was
going to try harder.

"I've never thought," I started to say, but he spoke over
me. He said, "It would never occur to them to help a relative
in need, and they have so much." He looked back at me, his
round face and nylon jacket shining in the porch light. It was
January. There was snow on the ground and the lake had
frozen. We had seen several deer in an opening in the woods.

I said, "I've never thought of you as anything but
generous."

It wasn't true. I had seen resentment in his eyes and
allowed that to govern me, so that I kept certain things secret,
certain small successes, and wouldn't meet his eye when he
talked about work.

Johnny, in the light from the porch, after seeing the five
deer grazing on low grass and weeds. He said sometimes he
saw them through the bedroom window when he woke up in
the morning. He said they travel in groups in the winter. He
had never seen five of them together in the summer.

I stood beside him until the deer moved into the woods,
then we walked on. Sometimes my gaze flitted past his,
sometimes I looked hard at him in order to not look at all,
but I couldn't fail to see that sadness had changed the look on
his face to one more open. His face was wiped with sadness
the way a floor is wiped with wax.

The path narrowed. He walked ahead, I followed. He
had put on a great deal of weight in a new marriage less
happy than expected after the lavish wedding, the prolonged
honeymoon, the general expectation that Lee would be
pregnant in a month or two. But ten months had gone by.

"I have protective instincts, aggressive instincts, but not generous ones," he said.

He could have been talking about me, I knew that. It even occurred to me from the way he looked at me so intently, that he was playing up a flaw in himself in order to point out the same flaw in me.

Six months went by, it was July, and my husband was saying, "You love to feast on the dark things that happen to people."

We were camping in a hot, dusty, still state park, the grass burnt brown, the trees lovely where they were, but not enough of them. I'm getting an ice cream for Annie, he said, taking our little girl to the ice cream truck. They came back and Annie was licking an ice cream and so was Ted. Sorry. I didn't ask if you wanted one, do you want one? Now that it's too late to get you one?

What he said was true. I relished every dark detail and wanted to talk about nothing else: how in turning to pour Johnny a cup of tea I had noticed the bandage on his arm. Haven't I told you? he asked, knowing he hadn't and turning faintly red while his eyes went soft with misery.

I said, "Their year started with such promise and has ended so badly."

"Good things happened too," insisted Ted.

He refused to encourage me. Refused to take heart, as I did, from their misfortune. Refused to believe it was misfortune. I couldn't stop thinking about them. Couldn't stop imagining, with a perverse sort of empathy, how they must feel. Pulled into their lives even as my feelings disqualified me from friendship.

What I felt was a puritanical pleasure at seeing this golden couple go through hard times, a primeval envy satisfied by the primeval obstacle in their way: They couldn't make a baby.

"Your heart was so set on it," I said to Johnny.

"I have other hearts," he said, and I could see from his eyes that he was protecting himself from me.

At every attempt to talk about them, I met my husband's disinclination and finally his smile. "You love to feast on the dark things that happen to people."

Does it show? I wanted to know. If it's so obvious to you, is it obvious to them?

All weekend I read Colette. I read the line, "the cool freshness between four and eight o'clock in the morning," then felt the truth of it, waking up cold about five and remaining cold under the single sheet until seven. This despite the tremendous heat all day and most of the night. Colette must have stayed up all night at times, or gone to bed very late, or risen very early. Or perhaps these were things everyone knew then, every rural person and even many city people.

In the morning I kept reading. I sat with my back to the domestic fatigue of tents, packing, quarrelsome children and dust, and looked out at the trees on the low hill and down at the words on the page: a story set in Paris, a beautiful woman of forty-five who has little money, but manages, although her future looms ahead as one of profound loneliness in the face of which her courage sometimes fails. There were various truths in the story, things that were simply said. "She was splendid in attack, but inclined to lose her head when she was on the defensive." I had been thinking only minutes before that I liked conflict, I liked to pick fights, but was too inarticulate to win them and too touchy to emerge unscathed.

And because I was inarticulate and edgy, and afraid people wouldn't like me, and angry, and afraid people would sense my anger, I tied myself into knots about things that ought to be straightforward.

But what is straightforward about wishing the worst for your friends? And what is straightforward about having your husband turn away repelled?

"It's what I most dislike about you," he said.

I said I wasn't crazy about it either.

By day I went over friendships, all their failings and pitfalls, and by night I dreamt of reconciliation, conversation, the gentlest affection. Maureen one night, Johnny the next. There was such a mood of relaxed peacefulness in those dreams, or in that part of the dream where it turned: Johnny turned to ask me a question, then said, "You know I've always felt the same way about you." He meant he had always felt a steady regard.

In the same dream Lee claimed to like what I had in my hand. There was nothing in my hand. "What do you mean?" I asked her, and she couldn't say. I complained about her insincerity to Johnny, who replied that you can't always say what you mean, you don't always know. Then it occurred to me that she might have meant the light in my hand. I held up my hand to see how the light fell on my empty palm.

Lee was wearing a flowered print dress with a strand of pearls. I kissed her on the cheek before telling her that she looked admirably serene. Such a thing to say to a troubled woman. She answered that she too was very sad, in fact she found the situation so hard that she was driven to make sense of it in some way. She said this without any alteration to her smile.

The restaurant had many tables and a view of the garden across the street. The windows were large and clean. People could see us as we bent over our soup.

Tell the truth, I kept thinking as I listened to her. But I didn't expect the truth. I expected what I got: the smile, the polish, the charm.

Delicate ill will. My suspicions reminded me of a flower – something petalled, present, so softened by other feelings that it seemed benign.

Outside we said goodbye. She turned right, I turned left only to go back after several blocks because I had forgotten my umbrella. I went back through the same glass door and scanned the restaurant just as I had scanned it upon arriving, but more quickly. I looked for the table, the chair, any sign of a telltale handle. It wasn't there, but Lee was. She had been in too much of a hurry to order coffee. Now she had a cup in front of her.

It was something I had never had the nerve to do: rid myself of a friend before going back to drink coffee in peace. My umbrella was hanging on a potted plant beside the cash register. I picked it off the branch and left, taking with me the image of Lee's small flowered back, recovering from me.

Johnny's Smile

Lawn chairs were arranged in the shade as they were every year, food was piled high, children were tearing around with watermelon in their fists and dogs at their heels. It was the annual summer picnic given by Johnny and Lee. All day they took pains to appear untroubled, and if they alluded to their problems it was always in the most lighthearted way. This seemed very American to me.

They had failed to invite certain friends I had bumped into a few days before – "Did you get an invitation this year?" they wanted to know. "Are you going?" – and I mentioned them to Johnny. He said of course they were welcome, when you've been invited once you're always invited. But no one was fooled. The people who came varied each year, some fell away without a word, lost at sea, never heard from again.

Ted tried to reassure me. He said, "Johnny's incapable of being offended about anything."

Whereas I thought he was capable of being offended by many things. I saw him as an easygoing man who was deeply competitive, an easily hurt man quick to rid himself of anyone who hurt him, a deeply disappointed man who refused to allow anyone to revel in his disappointment. A proud and friendly man who used friendliness to keep people at bay. Which one of us was right? Or did we simply bring out Johnny's different qualities, so that with Ted he was someone who never took offence and with me he was the opposite? Was it a matter not of finding out the truth about Johnny, but rather taking note of how he changed depending on whom he was with?

You absorb someone and he comes out someone else, made again, and yet he still stands, the one who existed before you ever met him, right there across from you. And these two people, the one you can't ever know and the one you think you know, become a large uncertainty. At best you are filtering parts of him through parts of yourself. Sometimes you filter his kindness through your envy, sometimes you filter his anger through your generosity, and each time you get a different person.

Over the years Johnny and I had had gusts of ill feeling followed by gusts of affection, the latter seeming to cancel out the former, but never a match for our mutual belief that neither of us had the other's interests at heart. In hindsight our affection always seemed paltry, nothing to depend upon, and ill will the only dependable thing.

Over berries a week later – washing them in an old metal colander – Jill and I talked about Johnny. She had known him longer and had seen the various stages of his life and the cast

of friends who changed with each stage. (Though she had
remained quietly constant and in the background – never so
valued as to become close, never so undervalued as to be left
behind.) Her fingers on the berries were jewelled. Always the
same six rings on the same six fingers. They weren't beautiful
rings, they were heavy and ornate, and her fingers weren't
beautiful either. They were too stubby, too white. A strange
habit, I thought, and asked her about it. She pointed to each
ring, naming who had given it to her, her hands clunky under
their load, but deft, and her logic always generous no matter
how sick she became. We were talking about Johnny's quick
and abiding displeasure despite his smiles, so that we were
never sure when the worm would turn. Once you're invited,
you're always invited; and he had immediately phoned the
uninvited friends. Naturally they hadn't come, though they
could have restored themselves only by coming, only by
some *effort*.

Jill said, "I know there are many things going on and I
also know that I'm always wrong."

She meant that in seeing Johnny's wounded, hurting,
complicated underside, she lost the breadth of his personality. She said her observations cut through his jolliness and
deepened him by reducing him. This paradox at the heart of
friendship baffled her.

Her kitchen was beautiful. All of the rooms in her house
were beautiful. The furniture was arranged, the various blues
and reds employed in ways that spoke of a natural artistic
bent. She wasn't obviously talented in the way Maureen was,
she hadn't excelled as a child or attempted anything ambitious as an adult, but she was not without ambition, not

without disappointment. She was rueful, generous, with a wider reach than her memorable sister. Maureen's conversation rarely strayed beyond herself, her children, and Danny. Jill was interested in you.

Even in sickness, especially in sickness, this remained the case.

"Feel my stomach," she said. I felt all the lumps – the way they pushed up like knobs, some small, some large – doorknobs under her skin.

A few weeks later she was in the hospital reading Mary McCarthy's *Cast a Cold Eye* (her husband had brought her the book), awful stories about marriage, she said, she couldn't understand why he had given them to her. And she related one about a woman who had a garden. The woman decided she would leave her husband after the petunias bloomed, and she did. But she had no plan. She called friends who all said they couldn't see her until the following week, or the week after that. So she stopped living – she went to movies – she did nothing until finally she went home again. The garden, when she opened the door, was full of weeds. She stood in the doorway, disbelieving, and her husband stood beside her. He said in a shocked voice, "Look how the weeds have taken over." Then he took her hand and said how much he loved the garden, or loved her in the garden, or loved the fact that she had loved the garden – something she knew to be a complete lie – but she didn't know what to say, and so she squeezed his hand in a false and outward show of emotion since nothing else occurred to her. She didn't know what else to do.

Jill lay in her hospital bed telling me the story in great detail, a story she said was too awful to read, and I listened, remembering it partially, the way I've recounted above, with the image in my mind of Jill's garden and the tall tomato plants her husband had pruned to within an inch of their lives.

Then I told her a painful story about my husband. An old friend of his, his colleague Rudy Jones, had been fired some months ago. Jill had never met Rudy, so I described him to her as plump, milky-faced, bone-lazy; a wonderful talker, funny, charming, eloquent, but less than useless when it came to work. Everyone except Ted said so. For a year he and Ted had shared the same office and the same views. Ted had covered for him, boosted his ego, talked him up to the other people at work. After Rudy was fired he blamed Ted for not quitting in protest, and dropped him cold. He dropped us both cold.

One night when Ted and I were sitting together in the living room after the kids were in bed, I said to him, "You always considered Rudy a closer friend than he considered you."

Ted said, "I guess you're right."

I was the one who expressed the anger he felt, then felt the anger he no longer wanted to feel. He spoke about Rudy only once. He said, "The biggest mistake I made in that job was to let my friendship with Rudy interfere with my judgement." That's all. He said it in passing.

His attitude mystified me. It seemed completely kind and good, a felicitous quality he had been born with. Things would come right, there was nothing bad that didn't have some good.

"And Hitler?" I asked him. "Show me the silver lining."

Yet I envied his steadiness – sanguine and very male – whose true value became apparent in friendship: he always saw the best in people, he always gave them credit. I, on the other hand, took friendships between my teeth and shook them the way my old dog shook snakes. Day after day I found myself rooted to the sidewalk shouting at Rudy in my head. The din was terrific. Through some perverse magnetism I had drawn to myself all the clatter and clamour and weaponry of male combat, I lumbered around under its weight while Ted walked free, neither angry nor remorseful nor stricken, but a friend.

"He'll come around," said Ted.

"No. He won't."

"In time."

"No. He'll never come around."

Ted remained reasonable (because I was so unreasonable. He was good because I was bad.)

I told Jill that I thought many women filled this role. They were vessels for their husbands' antipathy. They lost friends so their husbands could keep them, they slew the dragons of neglect so their husbands could feel benign. Then the husbands, witnessing the exhaustion of their wives under the burden of so much emotion, became patronizing. "Don't worry about it," they would say after their wives exploded disgracefully in public. And when pressed, "No. Your outburst didn't bother me." The wives would feel relieved, grateful not to be condemned for their lack of self-control, yet at the same time unsatisfied. All that emotion and so little response?

Jill said, "Ted must feel so hurt."

I said, "But I don't think he does. That's the point I'm trying to make."

Jill said, "Oh, oh. You and Mary McCarthy." Then she relented a bit. She generalized. She said, "I guess everybody misses the obvious sometimes."

I persisted. "He *looks* as if it doesn't bother him."

"You can't go by looks," said Jill. "Hasn't anybody ever told you that?"

It wasn't long after this that I had my sudden, long-overdue illumination. The sun was shining, the air was cool and dry, and I was standing beside Ted on the corner of Amsterdam and 105th while the traffic whizzed by. Ted said for the second time, quietly, and staring out at the traffic, "Rudy will come around." I looked at him and the following words dropped into my head: *He uses optimism to shield himself from pain.*

He'll come around didn't mean, I have faith in him and in the strength of our friendship. It meant, *I don't want to think about him because it's too painful. I've put him out of my mind.*

What had seemed a gift – the gift of eternal friendship – now seemed like an exquisitely-arrived-at means of survival.

The Chinese smile. The Eskimo smile. Johnny's smile. For a moment, basking in my revelation on the corner, I floated above Ted and Johnny, and even Rudy. I looked down through their smiles into a cross-section of everything that might have caused them pain and joy. It was the sort of view that appears in storybook illustrations of woodland dwellings or in a doll's house. I thought: this is how I should visit friends: like a fly on the wall, or a benevolent cloud.

That year Jill spent almost as much time inside the hospital as out. One afternoon when I was visiting her, Johnny came into her room with gifts. He brought *The Lover*, "Little books are best," and a muskmelon, "So are little melons," which he sliced up with a jackknife and handed around. He sat there grinning and chewing, a happy sloppy grin that you'd walk miles to see.

"Have you read it?" he asked her. She hadn't. It was one of the few books (she was a librarian, remember) that she had never read.

"You see," he said. "Today's my lucky day."

She wanted to know what it was about, and he said a girl from a crazy French family in Vietnam has a rich lover in a black car. They meet on a ferry and have to keep their affair secret, since she is fifteen and white and he is much older and Vietnamese. He said the key to *The Lover* was pacing: Duras took you to the river and onto the ferry, and you didn't know what was happening and then you did. I said I thought the key to the book was distance. No matter how close Duras was to what was happening, or how removed, she never got in her own way. Getting the right distance is the ticket, I said.

Jill held the little book, I sat in a padded green chair beside her bed, Johnny sat on the foot of the bed. His smile was like sunshine that day, at peace with me and with everything inside him. For an hour, while we kept Jill company, we had nothing to hide or be ashamed of.

A few months later Jill was back in the same hospital, but not in the same room. This time she didn't have a view. "What do you do," I asked her, "when you aren't giving the doctors a hard time?"

She said, "I choose a day from the past and relive it."

"Any day?"

"Always the same day. I never change a detail. It was a beautiful day in September. Maureen went off to boarding school and my grandfather gave me his ring."

After Johnny told Jill that he and Lee couldn't have a baby, Jill said to me, "It's like a death in the family. A tragedy." We were having lunch in her kitchen and I felt pushed aside by her compassion. She studied my face for a moment, then took my hand. "Don't worry. They'll be fine."

Thinking back, it doesn't seem so wrong that I spared myself in her presence. Spared her of my worst self. She would never have believed me anyway. She would have said, "You're so hard on yourself. Why are you so hard on yourself?" Which always seems to me to miss the point. I wouldn't be hard on myself if there was nothing to be hard about. Why is there so much to be hard about?

So I smiled. I smiled, and she said, "I've always loved your smile. You and Johnny," she said. "You have the best smiles."

Hand Games

It must have had a small, almost invisible beginning, or else I was so intent on believing that nothing was the matter that I missed it. I remember my growing sense of dismay, and my almost constant inner refrain that children are resilient. And I remember one afternoon that came to seem like the beginning, not of the bad time but of my awareness of the bad time.

I was walking down the street ahead of my daughter Annie and her friend Joyce. We paused many times. Joyce was wearing black patent leather shoes, and every hundred yards she bent down to dust them off. The shoes were tiny and new, and she dusted them with a white handkerchief. She was very small for four. Annie was the same age but much taller and puppy-like.

We weren't far from home. The street was lined with old trees, the sidewalk was yellow with leaves. I was carrying a bag of groceries in my right hand. Just before we got to the corner, I felt Joyce's small hand slide into my free hand, leaving the other one for Annie.

The game unfolded. Annie took my encumbered hand. For a while she said nothing, then whimpered – insisted – that I put the bag in my other hand. I told her not to be silly. Joyce said nothing. She'd said nothing when she ran ahead of Annie to slide her hand into mine, creating this deliberate, wordless, artful triangle.

The two girls were dressed in yellow and pink, and yet they reminded me of dark illustrations in an old storybook. *Dwarf with Dog* would be the caption. I saw my daughter gambolling at the feet of a tiny, dark, compact master. I saw myself in my daughter and my mother in myself – a long and sorry line of tailwagging.

That morning on the front steps Joyce had kept one hand in her bulging pocket.

Annie asked, "What's in your pocket?"

"Nothing."

"Tell me."

"*Nothing.*"

I lay awake at three in the morning and my daughter's face floated up, the moment when the two girls were coming down the stairs of Annie's school. We'll make hot chocolate, I said to them. Annie turned to Joyce and with a bright smile asked if she wanted hot chocolate. Joyce responded in a low voice. I was ahead of them and didn't catch the words. I caught the tone. I turned and saw my daughter's face widen, a pond into which a stone had been thrown.

We walked home. For a while they played, and then Annie asked for her toy phone. She held out her hand and Joyce walked over with it. A foot away Joyce stopped, put the phone to her own ear, turned her back, and began to talk to Wendy and Peter Pan. Annie lay on the sofa holding a doll to her chest. I saw her face wiped clean, glassy, the outermost reaches of the ripple. And did nothing.

Immobilized by the snake – the touch of the snake – the knowledge that someone can turn against you when you've done nothing wrong; the cavalier nature of friendship; the arbitrary nature of dislike; the twist of rejection; the fall from grace. All of these were present in that small configuration in the dark living room: one child lying on the sofa with averted eyes, the other talking into the toy phone, her back turned.

I did nothing. I didn't know what to do. I was afraid to scold Joyce because she was the daughter of an old friend.

Small hand in mine: soft warm devious hand brushing against mine as though with affection and need. I felt my palm mapped with her ill intentions, implicated in the betrayal of my daughter, pulled into the small child's canny vindictiveness – an intricate, serious, unhappy world. I played along with her even as I saw the game, drawn into the sophisticated world of the smaller child. Impressed by it.

Impressed by the meticulous words she was able to print, by the drawings, complex with colour and minute shapes. Seduced by the seriousness of the child, and intimidated.

Dwarf. Child/adult simultaneously. The interruption of a natural progression. We see a dwarf and are transfixed by the sight of adulthood in the form of a child forever estranged from adulthood, and we look away embarrassed and afraid.

Annie comes home. She comes through the door, hangs on the knob, leans into the door and then into me. She says, "Joyce did everything to hurt my feelings," and her face finally runs with tears.

It wasn't always this way. We moved into the building in September (drawn by the presence of these old friends, Joyce's parents) and for two months their friendship flourished in a form of Eden. The bad time – the first and worst bad time – began in November and went on for two months. Joyce would run to her small rocking chair and hiss, "This chair is my chair, this chair is my chair," low enough so that her mother couldn't hear but loud enough so that Annie heard, so that I heard – the woman who did nothing. She planted her tiny feet and stretched her arms across the hallway to bar Annie's passage. She pounced on Annie's mistakes. "That's not a jumping, it's a jumper. That's not a bicycle, it's a tricycle. That's not a skirt, it's a kilt."

At night Annie lay in bed under Joyce's bedroom and listened to the sounds above. She wrapped her handkerchief around her hand pretending it was broken. She breathed on the window, then drew a heart in the moisture and said, "I'm drawing a heart for Joyce."

Joyce likes to fold towels and pillow cases. I've watched her make the corners meet precisely and smooth the surfaces.

She builds neat piles and guards them. After any trip, no matter how short, she goes into her bedroom and touches all the stuffed animals. Her mother has told me this. I suspect she doesn't have names for them, she isn't fanciful in that way, but she likes them. When her sisters throw them off the shelf, I've seen her grab the nearest arm and pinch. She gets punished but she doesn't seem to mind this kind of punishment: the sister removed, the door closed, the silence. She puts the animals back on the shelf, always in the same order: soft blue donkey with faded ribbon, rougher older larger bear, white owl, grey rabbit, brown rabbit, cloth rabbit, white lamb, purple hippo – blue, brown, white, grey, brown, pale yellow, white, purple. She arranges colours in her drawings with the same care. When anyone compliments her on her drawings, and they often do, she doesn't acknowledge the compliment. And she never holds up a drawing to say look at this.

Annie puts her hand in mine and feels the hard ridge of plastic, the reduced space for her own hand, the weight of groceries pulling my arm down, my quick step; and there is Joyce, on the other side, with my free hand all to herself.

The softest part of my hand is the palm and the hardest part is the bottom of the fingers. They are the hardest and coldest part. Annie tells me, "My skin is soft and your skin is hard."

She brushes against my leather jacket and looks down at the sidewalk which is uneven and dusty. People pass by and say of Joyce, "How adorable, is she yours?" "No," I say, "she's a friend."

Annie tries to take Joyce's hand. Sometimes Joyce lets her, sometimes she tightens her hand into a fist, or jerks her hand away, or pushes Annie away.

We walk up the steps to our building. We rent the first floor, Joyce's family has the second, a family with three boys lives on the third, an old couple on the fourth, a woman with her daughter on the fifth. Six wide steps lead up to the blue front door. At the top of the steps, Joyce and Annie scramble for the wealth of menus left by all the Chinese restaurants in the neighbourhood. Joyce gets four, Annie gets two. "Inside you'll share them," I say.

In the kitchen Joyce slides into Annie's chair and says, "I'm the guest."

Annie looks at me. I look away and say yes, that's right, Joyce is the guest.

Increasingly, I have been feeling the weight of Joyce's jacket. It is soft, bright pink, a year old. The weather has turned cold. Today I ask Joyce if she would like to wear her coat and she gives a fierce shake of the head. I drape the coat over the back of the stroller in which the baby is sleeping, and we walk across the street to get Annie. The girls go to different schools, and twice a week I pick up Joyce as well as Annie.

In the hallway I button up Annie's coat, adjust her hat and say to Joyce, "You can wear the coat or you can put it over your arm but you have to carry it."

Joyce is holding one of her drawings, she says she can't carry her coat as well.

"Put the drawing in the stroller then." And I reach for it.

Joyce steps back. Refuses.

"You have to carry your coat, Joyce. Each of us is responsible for her own coat. I'm not going to carry it."

I know the coat could be shoved easily into a corner of the stroller, or draped over the back. But I am irritated because my ploy hasn't worked and because I am using a ploy. Now that the train of events has been set in motion, it will play itself out in full.

I insist. Joyce refuses. I take the coat, which has a hood, and drop the hood over Joyce's head. We set off. I have to buy vegetables. Half way down the block Joyce is crying, darkly furious and on the verge of a tantrum, that the coat is slipping off her, that she has to hold her picture. Outside the vegetable store, she lets the jacket fall to the sidewalk. A passerby picks it up and hands it to me, and I drop the hood over her head. By this time she is storming – loud piercing cries, choked sobs – that her mother never makes her do this – her mother always puts her coat on the stroller – my mother – sob – my mother . . .

I bend down, by now trembling, and tell her that I don't care what her mother does, nor does her mother do that; if she doesn't carry her coat – I hear myself say – there won't be any hot chocolate.

"I don't want hot chocolate," she screams.

"I don't care what you want, I am not carrying your coat."

I push the stroller on, and with trembling fingers choose from the outdoor display four tomatoes, three green peppers, a bunch of parsley. Joyce stands in full tantrum in the middle of the sidewalk, the jacket on the ground except for one sleeve which she holds in her hand. I push the stroller inside the store, my daughter follows, so does Joyce.

"What's the matter?" someone asks.

"Nothing's the matter," I answer. "She doesn't like her coat."

The cashier smiles sympathetically, but I don't care if the cashier is sympathetic. I pay. The children and the coat follow me back outside. Joyce drags it, but she doesn't leave it behind.

Sickness and holidays intervene, and two weeks pass before I pick up Joyce again. I climb the stairs to her school, pick up her lunchbox and coat, and we go downstairs together. At the door I hand Joyce her coat, then bend down to see to my son in the stroller. I say, "Joyce, you can wear your coat zipped up or unzipped. Which is it going to be?"

Joyce stands by the door, coat in hand, looking down. I feel the ground give way as I face this dark child.

"Zipped or unzipped?"

"Unzipped," she says, and puts it on.

It is bitterly cold. The coat slides off her shoulders and blows wide in the wind.

"Are you cold?" I ask. She shakes her head. "I can zip it up for you." Shake of the head.

We pick up Annie from her school and walk several blocks. Joyce is shivering and nothing is said. Annie starts to talk about her approaching birthday. She will be five. Joyce has already had her birthday, three weeks back.

Then Joyce speaks. She says to Annie, "I'm not coming to your birthday and I'm not giving you a present."

Annie looks at me – slow motion towards tears – and I bend down and speak to Joyce. You have had your birthday and now Annie is going to have hers; you can't say mean things about it; apologize. Joyce is also close to tears. She says she is sorry. Then as I stand up she says something else, softly. The look on Annie's face makes my question sharp. "What did you say, Joyce?"

"My mother says I don't have to come."

I try to remember what it was like to be lost in such obstinacy. Some days I can remember and some days I can't.

My friendship with Joyce's mother has changed. I lie awake at night talking to her, but in person I say nothing. At night I tell her that I can't stand it any more. I ask her what we should do. Old scenes between Joyce and Annie play out in my mind. But I know Norma has plenty of problems and doesn't need more. And I'm afraid that once I start to recount what Joyce has done to Annie, our friendship will never be the same. But it isn't the same now. We talk to each other, ignoring our daughters, pretending these things aren't happening, and each of us is glad when the other leaves.

Joyce makes our friendship unsustainable, and yet it continues. I continue to pick up Joyce out of loyalty to Norma, and out of my inability to find phrases for what I feel.

Other children live on the block. Linnea lives across the street. She and Joyce have been going to the same school since they were two. Later Linnea's role in the story will become clear to me. It is always clear to Annie.

Annie continues to say, "Joyce is my *best* friend, right? Joyce is my *best* friend."

At her insistence, I take her by the hand up the flight of stairs to Joyce's apartment. Norma answers the door, I ask her if Joyce would like to play.

Norma turns to her daughter. "Would you like to go down?"

"No." The answer is no.

I smile. "Another time."

I hurry Annie away, not up another flight to find another playmate and teach her about the possibility of other friends, the importance of going on, but downstairs and inside. To be especially kind? No, especially irritated. Angry. At being reminded of my own childhood and forced to realize it will happen again.

I begin to invent excuses: they're not home; it's suppertime; they're out of town.

I pretend to phone, dialling with one finger and holding the receiver down with the other. "They're not home," I say.

After a few days, enough time so that Annie won't seem to be begging for friendship, I give in and we go upstairs.

The staircase is carpeted and wide. Annie's right hand holds the wooden railing – cool and hard and smooth – and we walk up into the smell of cooking from the floors above, and down the hall to Joyce's door.

"Ring the bell," says Annie.

I reach up and ring it, and I hear Joyce's voice. "Linnea, Mom! It's Linnea!"

Joyce swings the door open and Norma appears at her side. Behind them is Joyce's special tea set, pink and new and never brought out for Annie to play with. Quickly, "Would Joyce like to come down to play, or do you have other plans?"

Norma hesitates. Then, "Annie can stay and play, I don't mind."

Annie, already inside, stays.

It wasn't possible – why wasn't it possible? – for Norma to say that she had invited Linnea to play. It wasn't possible for me to say what I knew, and that we would come back another time.

An hour later I returned for Annie. Linnea was there, and Linnea's mother.

Joyce said to Annie, "You can go now."

Norma reproached her. "Now, Joyce."

This had been going on the whole time.

"There are different things you can do," I say to Annie. "You can tell her to stop being mean. You can tell her you don't like it. You can walk away and climb into a chair and read a book."

She has come down from upstairs. She has stopped crying. She is on the sofa leaning her head against my shoulder.

A few hours later I tuck her into bed and she says, "Talk to me more about Joyce."

"About what you can do?"

"Yes."

"Well, you can just walk away from her and play on your own."

She doesn't say anything. She is holding my hand. Then, "I don't want you to pick up Joyce anymore."

I look out the window. A yellow taxi is parked across the street and I think of some tragedy, nothing specific, just the general idea of something unbearable and how I might react. The disbelief, finding myself in a situation recognizable from literature, saying to myself – this is Shakespearean. A misunderstanding of such proportions, an incident so earthshattering, as to make one's life like a book worth reading. The thought injects a certain distance, and the distance a certain relief.

But five-year-olds aren't Shakespearean. They can't even read.

2

On the last day of January I come home, insert my key in the first door to the apartment – the apartment has two doors at either end of a long hallway – and see the farther door swing shut. I go still. Ted is at work, no one is home.

I open the door, look the length of the apartment, and see no one. I find a neighbour on the third floor and together we look through the apartment. I go outside. I see another neighbour and tell her, and once more we comb the apartment. But there is no one. No explanation.

Later I mention it to a friend.

"You saw the future," he says.

What I saw was a triangle of pink: the triangle formed by the doorway and the closing door, and the colour mysterious because the door was brown and the paint in the kitchen was white.

In the afternoon I heard a child's voice in the hallway and felt dismay. Listened – no. Listened – yes. Linnea. Linnea was going upstairs to play with Joyce. I felt such pity, such mortified sadness for my daughter who hadn't been invited. I was transfixed by the pattern repeating itself from childhood. In having a daughter I had rubbed my own childhood into view, and was still rubbing, bent over that worn engraving and rubbing it into view – a picture that emerged through touch rather than sight, and in that way of childhood: knees on the floor, busy fingers, paper and pencil.

I wrote to my mother. In passing I mentioned Joyce. You remember, the aloof and solitary child with a mean streak. I said I had almost come to hate her. That's all.

But as I wrote, my own relationship with my mother – that awkward unhappy thing – came back to mind. My own refusal to please. How else could it be described? I used to sit on the verandah steps and deliberately withdraw. I knew that I had a choice. I could laugh when I was teased and win my parents' approval and my mother's gratitude, or I could sulk and fume. I chose to sulk, though that isn't the best word to describe the combination of fury and helplessness and pleasure which I chose to inhabit because it satisfied me more than cheerfulness, especially cheerfulness as practised by my mother – an unfailing attitude, a permanent posture. With my mother, pleasing and pleasure were the same.

My mother wrote back. I'm sorry, she said. I caught her tone, the shake of the head, the unspoken "It's a shame." An end-of-the-world tone, useless, completely useless to me.

Where does it come from, this end-of-the-world thinking? The belief that one bad thing cancels out everything else? It must be the panic of childhood retained. So that in the face of one criticism everything else, everything positive, the continuous ground we stand upon, falls away. A slight by Joyce of Annie, a criticism of my husband by a colleague, and the world drops away.

Why do some people retain the sense of a continuous world around them, and others not?

I ask Joyce to wait in her cubby, and I go into the teacher's office which is off to one side. I say, "I need some advice."

The teacher asks me if I have talked with Norma. I shake my head. "She's a dear friend, I'm picking up Joyce to help her out." I shake my head again.

"You may have to," says the teacher, "but there are two other things you can do. You can say to them, 'You don't have to like each other all the time, you don't have to play with each other all the time, but you do have to be nice to each other.' And you can separate them. Put one of them to play by herself in one room, and the other in another room."

The teacher's voice is very loud. I move to close the door tightly, and the teacher continues to talk just as loudly. Doesn't she care if Joyce hears? Does she want her to know she is being talked about? Does she think that will help? She says that little girls, especially, are like this.

We finish talking and I leave her office. Joyce is still sitting in her cubby, her face sombre and unreadable. We go down the stairs and across the street to Annie's school. Every few feet of our progress, I congratulate myself that things are going smoothly, that I am calm, that I haven't given Joyce any rope to hang me with.

The teacher said, "Your daughter needs your protection. You must interfere."

I say to both children, "We have a new rule. You don't have to play together, but you have to be nice to each other." And I set up two spots, the rocking chair where Joyce can sit by herself, the sofa for Annie.

When they quarrel I try something I read in a book. I ask each of them to tell me what's the matter. Annie tells me. Joyce won't. I guess what's the matter with Joyce and she nods. Then I tell them to go and sit on my bed. "Close the door, talk it out for five minutes, come back with a solution."

I am amazed when they come back smiling and tell me what they have decided.

I watch them sometimes through the glass door, conferring on the bed. They sit side by side, as though on a park bench, and sometimes they come back after a few minutes and sometimes they remain. But the problem, the quarrel, goes away.

In a few weeks they are closer friends than they have ever been.

They play house, castle, boat, pirate ship, camping. They pull around the furniture in the living room, drape it with old pieces of material, add the little table and chairs from Annie's bedroom; they erect walls with square pieces of old foam, and fashion a rooftop from a long flat cushion. The little areas they make are small and beautiful, and often so carefully arranged with pieces of old black lace and rose-covered fabric that they look Japanese. The two of them in combination, not alone, make these places and play quietly for hours.

These little tents of friendship – creative and flimsy, improvised from big and little, different each time – have enough space for just the two of them; they sit under the shelter of an old shawl roof and pour themselves pretend tea.

I watch them become friends again, unable to put my finger on how it happens and aware that everything might crumble again.

It does. Once again Joyce turns against Annie.

It happens one afternoon after two hours of happy playing. Joyce fights with one of her sisters and is sent to her room. But it is Annie she insults. From her bed she yells, "Annie Pinhead." And again. "Annie Pinhead!"

Annie hears her. She smiles and walks towards me. A tentative half-smile that doesn't last.

Norma goes into Joyce's room, pulls her out into the kitchen and tells her to apologize. She won't. Her mother shakes her. She still won't.

"You'll apologize tomorrow then," and she pushes her back towards her room.

On the outs. It's almost a crack down the side of your body, a shade you occupy while others sit in the sun. A dark brassiness, metallic, exposed, abandoned to the weather. And yet you choose it, and not just because it's familiar. You formulate plans – not plans of action, plans of emotion.

The streetlight comes on and I imagine Joyce raising her gaze. She looks out the window at Linnea's house and pictures a special tea party, just the two of them, with ice cream and real tea and sugar cubes.

Someone she recognizes – Matthew's mother – goes into Linnea's house. Linnea has been playing with Matthew, and now he is coming out with his mother. Tall skinny Matthew has been playing with tall skinny Linnea.

Her mother comes into the room. She is urgent, emphatic, determined, worried. "You can't treat your friends that way, or you won't have any friends."

But Joyce knows this isn't so. She knows that Annie will always come running.

3

My mother comes to visit. One evening she helps Annie with her homework. I lie on the sofa and listen to her soft relentless voice. "What does this say? Sound it out. What sound does this letter make? What letter is it? What sound does it make?"

The soft patience which at any moment will turn sharp. And here it is. "How did you get *that*?"

Annie begins to chew on her hand. She puts the side of her thumb into her mouth, then the side of her hand, making small wet teeth marks. Her grandmother says, "Don't," and pushes her hand out of her mouth. "It will get sore."

I look at the furniture while this goes on. The light from the standing lamp falls through the mesh on the big armchair and makes a pattern on the soft velvet seat. I don't interfere any more than I interfere with Joyce. I listen, and relive my mother's voice directed similarly at me. The quiz, where the adult knows the answer and you don't. Where the adult pretends she is helping when, in fact, she is testing.

I hear my voice (it is my mother's voice) quizzing my daughter and my mother quizzing me – the pattern has splayed wider – and I feel pain on my child's behalf, and on my own behalf, and on my mother's behalf, since although she appears to be the source of this unreasonable and unnecessary unhappiness, how can she be? Someone came before her too.

In the morning I make coffee, and try to say something that Ted won't dismiss as extreme. I don't say that I feel as if I'm in the presence of evil. I don't say that Joyce is full of raw newborn malice. I say that Annie doesn't seem to have as much stamina as her two-year-old brother. Ted looks at me.

"Don't you remember?" he asks. "When Annie was two she had just as much stamina." And he describes the way she would get up at five in the morning and run around the kitchen with arms held high.

It comes back to me then, a vision of happy exuberance. I feel the size and weight of that plump little body, remember the expressions on her face, the irrepressible personality. Bright, tough, funny, tender. Now, three years later, here she is. Taller, skinnier, and burdened, somehow, with temperament.

"Her life is much harder and more complicated now," he says. "She's much more aware of the world out there, and she has friendships to deal with."

A phrase goes through my mind. The stress of friendship. How early that kicks in.

When I finally react, I overreact. Perhaps it's because so many peaceful months have gone by. Perhaps that's why I can't bear the next falling out. It's summer. School has ended. The two girls haven't seen each other for two weeks because my daughter has chosen a day camp that offers swimming, and Joyce doesn't want to swim. Annie hasn't asked to see Joyce until now. She goes upstairs to play, and after twenty minutes comes back. "Joyce told me to leave," she says. And the tears begin.

For the next two weeks Joyce is deliberately cold and punitive. Annie is pensive, but how unhappy it's hard for me to say. I am fierce. I tell Annie that Joyce is not welcome in our home. I say, "Her sort of behaviour isn't allowed."

Ted objects. "Are you sure it's wise?"

But I am strident, determined. Annie has to learn to steel herself. She has to learn what I was never taught. She has to learn not to be taken for granted.

Annie wants to know if we are never going to invite Joyce again.

"Not until she invites you," I say. "Let her take the first step. I won't allow you," I say, "to invite her."

Several times over the next week Annie broaches the subject. We will be in the street and she will say, "We're never going to invite Joyce?" Then she will say that Joyce is her oldest friend and she is Joyce's oldest friend. "We knew each other since we were babies. We've been friends since we were one year old, two years old, three years old, four years old, five years old. Joyce and Linnea are just friends since they started going to school." She is building a faith as she skips along beside me.

We pass a fruit store and she is framed by fresh tomatoes, oranges, the first strawberries. I look down at her and see her trying to soften and reassure me. My attempt to harden her makes her even softer. She is handling me the way she handles Joyce.

A few days later Joyce initiates a visit and it goes completely smoothly, as does almost every visit after that.

When I think back on the whole period, I know that most of the time – eighty percent of the time – the two girls were fast friends. A pattern of intimacy controlled and periodically broken by Joyce. I don't know whether they adjusted to each other or whether Annie adjusted – gave way – to Joyce. Whatever happened was invisible and miraculous and temporary. They would be down by the river, fishing out leaves, nuzzling a lunch of orange slices on a blanket – grazing, I thought, as I heard their wet little mouths working – and I would be impressed by their diplomacy and affection, by the simplicity and sophistication of their forgiveness. I would feel relieved and wary. Months would go by without a break, months when the friendship was the most stable part of their lives and whatever troubles they had they resolved themselves. And then something would happen.

What happened, I realize, was always the same. Joyce would pull away and Annie would wait for her to come back.

"I wait for the other day," she told me.

"For another day?"

"Yes. She says she's never going to be my friend, and the next day she's my friend again."

One child knew all about power and the other learned all about patience.

I should have expected the final trouble, but it took me by surprise. A cool summer preceded this last episode. One morning Norma came down with a bag of clothes. All week she had been packing and setting aside warm things as unnecessary. Joyce was on her heels. She insisted on keeping several things and uncharacteristically her mother gave in. Suddenly there was an area of yielding that hadn't been there before, an eagerness to compensate for all the upheaval. They were moving south.

I watched Joyce enter this new emotional territory. Her grandmother catered to her more than ever, her parents softened their criticism, friends made arrangements to see her for the last time; they brought gifts, they cried. It seemed to me that Joyce enjoyed the narrowing of focus, the paring away of possessions, the simplifying of life even as it became more complicated. This was a process she was adept at, riding a storm in a narrow and purposeful boat.

That summer my daughter learned several hand games. She played them fast and with tremendous merriment. There would be the slapping of palm against palm – knee – shoulder – palm in patterns that were ingenious and rewarding. Her face was brown, attentive, relaxed.

Joyce was good at not playing, at making you feel foolish for wanting to play.

This would be their final summer together.

Two days before they moved away, Norma and I talked about our daughters. It happened the morning after the going-away party, after Annie's confused sorrow and my relief that there would be no more of this. I walked upstairs and knocked on Norma's door.

Norma was packing. She listened and said, "I'm so sorry. I didn't know."

"It's not all bad," I said. "Annie has to learn how to protect herself. She has to learn not to wear her heart on her sleeve."

"But that's the wonder of her," said Norma, and she leaned against the doorway, slender and tired and worried.

Annie and I had left the going-away party early to sit on the lower bunk in her room. It was dark outside. The window was open, sounds from the party drifted down. It had been raining all day. Annie listened to my voice – low and hesitant – say that Joyce was about to move and would miss her very much. She didn't believe me. She said, "She won't even remember me because I didn't sign the book." And she cried quietly.

She meant the guest book. It was on a small table beside the large table of food, and friends had been writing down their names, addresses, sentimental farewells. For most of the party Joyce wouldn't speak to Annie. She wouldn't acknowledge her presence. Linnea was there, and several of Joyce's cousins. Even after Linnea left, even after the cousins went home, Joyce wouldn't speak to Annie or look at her.

"I know Joyce doesn't like me – she's sick of me – she didn't play with me all night – she won't even remember me because I didn't sign the book."

"You can sign the book tomorrow."

"She didn't even talk to me."

"You know what Joyce is like. You know how nasty she can be sometimes."

"I know she can be nasty, but I don't know *when*."

I sat on the edge of the bunk and didn't know what to do. Should we take Joyce's cue and not bother to say good-bye? Should we wait until moving day and expect her to say goodbye then? Should we let her define the friendship?

This last thought was the one that cut through my anger, and I heard myself suggest that Annie make a going-away card for Joyce.

"Would you like to?"

Annie said she would. The suggestion seemed to relieve her. She put her head on the pillow and fell asleep.

The next morning I went upstairs. My heart felt loose inside me and I said too much too apologetically. It shouldn't be so hard to be straightforward.

Around us was the chaos of the move. Norma was wearing a dress she had intended to give away, but under the stress of the move she had lost so much weight that it finally fit. It looked lovely on her and I said so.

"What should we do?" I asked.

"What if I made a time for the two of them to play together by themselves? Later this afternoon? I'll extend an invitation."

In the afternoon the sisters came down to invite Annie and her brother to watch a movie. They came down alone, then they came back with Joyce because they wanted to start the movie right away; they wanted Annie and her brother to hurry up.

"Hi, Joyce," Annie said with a small and hopeful smile.

Joyce didn't reply. She stood out in the hallway and looked away.

Annie waited a moment, then repeated, "Hi, Joyce."

Joyce, without looking at her, said hi.

Annie looked at me then with the same hopeful smile, but wider, even more hopeful, and full of relief. She was reassuring me that everything was all right.

The next day Joyce's family moved away. In the hour before their departure, Joyce and Annie played. Quietly, at first, and on the sofa. They sat side by side. Then they went outside onto the street where the moving van was being filled. They hung on the fence, they ran and scampered and laughed.

Just before they left, Norma gave me a card that Joyce had made for Annie but "forgotten" to give to her. Joyce didn't forget to show Annie Linnea's gift of writing paper. This she made a special trip upstairs to get; this she displayed, full of smiles; this she hugged to her chest.

Now I look up from grating a cabbage and see Norma through the window – same hair, same sweater. I start, and the woman catches sight of me and smiles. It's the sweater. A heavy dark brown and white sweater that Norma used to wear in the fall. And the loose thick hair.

I see Joyce too, but not in the same way, or in any way that I could have predicted. I see her in Annie.

A new family has moved in upstairs. One of the children is Annie's age and they are in the same class. In the morning the new girl, Marcela, runs up to Annie and Annie turns away.

Norma at the window, and Joyce in Annie – the absence of a smile, and something more than shyness.

I think of my mother, a woman with no protective shell. She is porous to everyone she meets, and this is difficult for them as well as for her. They feel invaded by an innocent country, she feels taken aback to learn that she isn't welcome. There is no end to her when she is with other people, no solitude. She wants, like a child, to be included and at the centre of everything. And yet this doesn't occur out of egotism, at least not of the usual kind, but out of friendliness; the egotism of the shy perhaps. Not that she is shy, but shyness shaped her, and the desire to be liked.

I have seen my mother treated the way Joyce treated Annie. Seen her greet someone with great friendliness, someone dark and shy and reserved and cruel, and seen that person not respond. Seen my mother repeat her cheery greeting more cheerily: "I said hello." And seen the response: "I know."

A cool and rude young man irked by her overeagerness. It wasn't just his coolness, his rudeness; it was her effort, her inability to be easy about friendship, her obvious need to have people like her. The new girl upstairs has this quality, this willingness to be hurt.

Joyce so small, so concentrated, with those hunting headlights in her eyes, and the highway so wide and dark. Her cruelty took the form of savage silences, calculated, cool, sophisticated. Women treat men this way – men they want to punish, men they want to keep.

"Such a mean streak," Norma said once.

And I softened it, reassured her. We all have mean streaks, she's not a mean child.

I lied. I hoped. I reassured. I misunderstood. I thought she was a child who didn't suffer fools gladly, a child driven by a principled refusal to please. In her cubby at school she never looked up. Other children raced around and shouted when their mothers and babysitters arrived. Joyce didn't. She wouldn't give me, wouldn't give her mother, the satisfaction of getting what we wanted. She saw the expectation in our faces, however muted, felt it in the stance of our bodies as we waited for her to stand up.

One morning I realized my mistake. I saw her in the schoolground during recess. Her teacher was carrying her on her hip while the other children ran around, and Joyce was playing up to her shamelessly. I had never seen her so happy.

They drove away finally. They moved. And just before moving Joyce took pains to remind Annie of who was boss. Don't ever think you don't need me, and don't ever think I need you.

Annie looks for mail every day. She pulls a chair into the hall and stands on it to reach the mailbox. When Joyce's postcard arrives – after days of waiting – Annie sticks it up on the refrigerator door. The postcard says how much Joyce misses her. This is what Annie wanted to hear, all she wanted to hear.

Annie writes a postcard to Joyce. "All I'm thinking about is you," she writes. Then says to me, "That's not all I'm thinking about, but that's okay."

A month later she draws a picture of our apartment – the long sofa, the window, the big round overhead light. She writes *shshshsh* across the bottom of the page because, she says, the people upstairs are saying *shhhh* and the cars outside say *shhhh* when it rains.

I suggest that she send the picture to Joyce but she doesn't want to.

"Would you like to write her a letter?"

No, she doesn't want to do that either. "I wrote to her already."

Joyce in Annie: a more determined child, no less easily hurt but eager to be someone. She sits at the table with her new friends and they compete over who has the most cousins, who has travelled farthest, who has plans to travel soon, and her small face runs with feeling. She shows everyone Joyce's postcard, even as a party we attend brings back memories of the going-away party and sparks the comment, "Joyce did that to me." We're standing beside a table of food, children are chasing each other through the rooms. "Joyce did that to me," she says. And then, "She was thinking she'd never see Linnea again."

"But why would that make her treat you badly?"

She doesn't answer. Later I ask again. "What made Joyce behave that way?"

"We talked about that already," her face flushed – embarrassed – private.

How different we are. Why has it taken me so long to realize? She has never believed that Joyce was mean for the sake of being mean. She has always seen the whole thing as an affair of the heart. She was to Joyce as Joyce was to Linnea.

I dream about my daughter. I have taken her to school, into a room crowded with children, and she won't stay. She follows me into the hallway where I scold her endlessly, all the while aware of what others are thinking. They are thinking, No wonder the child is so unhappy.

I see everything in stark terms – a child's capacity for evil, my incapacity to protect my child. I see a fatal flaw, something inherited that my mother and I have never been able to shake – a line of rejection passing down. But Annie (who has the clearest eyes, a man said, that he had ever seen) sees, instead, the nature of love.

Overnight Visitor

A friend arrived in the middle of a snowstorm. This happened fifteen years ago. She flew in from Vancouver and stayed with me over night, then continued on to Toronto the next day. I was living in Winnipeg at the time. My apartment wasn't far from Osborne Street, so at dinnertime we walked the few blocks to the bridge, crossed the river, and found a café just beyond the Country Style Donut Shop I went to every Saturday morning for coffee with double cream, one sugar. They used 18 percent cream, that's why their coffee was so good.

It was still blowing snow when we set out and by the time we reached the café we were frozen stiff. The café was on the second floor of a boutique of some sort and we sat at a tiny table beside a window, looking at each other and down at the snowy street.

My friend talked non-stop. (I may be intense, the odd person has told me I am, but I don't hold a candle to Bev.) Why do you like her? a friend asked me once. If I had been honest I would have said, because she likes me. I suspect I said that she was lively and loyal, and those things were true too. Her conversation was zany and relentless, full of theories that never made much sense. I thought to myself, it's only one night, it won't kill me, but I was glad when we were back outside where I could watch the snowploughs and escape her gaze. It was still very cold and I was looking forward to sleep.

Had I been simply straightforward, or plainly discouraging, nothing would have happened. Surely that's true. But there must have been some sexual slippage – enough play in the rope – that she felt encouraged. Because after we got home and I came out of the bathroom in my nightgown, she was in my bed. I had made up a bed for her on the couch in the living room, and she had pouted. "All alone? You're leaving me all alone?" Now she was saying, "We'll just keep each other warm." (It's getting light as I think about this. My daughter called a few minutes ago because she was cold. I put an extra blanket, folded double, on her bed.)

Getting light around the dark gusty leaves and above the dark rooftops. As has happened so often in my life, I went along. I climbed into bed and for a while we talked, then she put her hand on my breast.

I felt a certain inevitability and curiosity. What harm can it do? And no harm was done. I discovered different textures – the thinness of her lips, the sponginess of her breasts, the feel of flesh that gives way, falls in, offers no resistance. I must have slept. In the morning I got up and dressed. I expect I got up very early, just as now, and that she continued to sleep. In those days my kitchen table was blue. Now it's white. I must have tried to appear unalarmed. In this aspect there would have been no difference between the aftermath with her and the aftermath with a man. There was a difference though. Whether it was based on fear, or on anger veiled by friendship, I have never been able to say. Partly out of friendship, partly out of fear, I haven't been able to say, but I felt panic-stricken and I felt sick.

Bev was the one who threw up. She lay on the couch, too ill to move. I covered her with a blanket and she remained there, immobilized, until it was time to catch her plane. She was out of commission and I was safe. Sickness had come to my rescue.

Afterwards, gradually and then precipitously, and for a year, we were estranged. Precipitous when she came to visit and fondled my neck, and I told her to keep her hands to herself. She was wounded, but not in a straightforward fashion. She spoke very little for the next hour, and not at all for the next year. Easily done, since we lived in separate cities. Then her attitude softened. She began to call again, but without making any verbal passes, so that once again I relaxed. Now we speak to each other by phone once or twice a year, and she has gone back to her old ways. That is, she never lets me forget that she has sex on her mind.

Does she know something about me that I don't know? Something that allows her to think I'm fair game? Or is she this way with every woman she meets?

She feeds my doubts with friendship. The doubts grow fat and glossy, as does the affectionate hand that strokes them.

Now I can see the colour of the leaves. They are yellow and green, yellow on the outer edges, green where the sun doesn't penetrate. The wind is still blowing.

Where was friendship in all of this? Friendship was everywhere. That was the trouble.

❖

I left this story for a year because I didn't know how to continue. I could imagine someone saying: she touches upon her inhibition only to shift away.

October, and the temperature has dropped. I look out the window and never in my life have I seen such clarity. Every leaf, every stem, every blade of grass and shimmer of fence comes forward as if brought to my eyes by binoculars. The sky is so blue it could be water washed and hung out to dry. I take my boy to the park, and again I look at him as if through binoculars, but he is only a few feet away.

I haven't heard from Bev for over a year. This is unusual. She may be in love and very busy, or our last encounter may have killed all interest. Last September I travelled to her city on business. Such words grown-ups get to use. We travel *on business*. I called her. In fact I had written to say I was coming. I was there for three days, grateful for her friendship since my so-called business was even less momentous than my pessimism had prepared me for. I was at loose ends and feeling silly. So I was glad to be able to talk to her on the phone, and to visit.

Her apartment was tiny and marshmallowy. Fluffy. At least in memory. The furniture must have been pillowy and soft, the carpet thick. The two of us sat almost eye to eye in that little space. I was fascinated that she had a whole wall of videos, not a single one of which I wanted to see, and I like movies.

She was uncomplicated in her friendliness, except for once. She must have been telling me about her new lover (her first relationship in five years) who perhaps had only recently realized she was gay. Or perhaps the lover had known all along and this was the point: no more affairs, Bev may have said, with women who aren't sure. It was Bev's theory that many, many women, most of them married and famous, were actually lesbians. She would ream off names ranging from Anne Murray to Dinah Shore, and I would pull one face after another. Seriously, she would say, it's true. "How do you know?" She had read it, heard it somehow, and knew it to be true.

"And what about Bethie?" she asked me. "Is she gay?" She always called me Bethie.

I looked at her for a moment – at her eager, expressive, strangely youthful face. She always looked younger than she was because of her bouncing-ball sort of energy, even when she was exhausted from studying for yet another degree, yet another career. Strangely youthful, because more than anyone else I know she has had bad luck, a series of grim accidents that have caused great physical pain. The pain hasn't changed her face except to make it fleshier.

"No," I said.

There must have been something new about my *no*. I heard it myself: a matter-of-fact, not-to-be-budged, end-of-story tone to my voice.

"I think you're right," she said.

Whether right or not, I was glad to be left alone.

My daughter remembers her because several years ago, when she came to dinner, she read her palm. Only days ago Annie said, "Your friend who sees the future."

"You remember her," I said, and she said, "I'll never forget her."

Bev would be pleased.

"What do you remember?"

"I remember her father was a fortune teller and he told fortunes to get girls."

"You mean to get them to go out with him?"

"Yes. She said I would have a long life, and that I'd die just like that and not suffer. And she said my love line is very deep."

"What does that mean?"

Annie, sitting in her nightgown on the foot of my bed, scrunched her knees up to her chin. "Affectionate, I think."

Twenty years ago Bev told my fortune too, a reading that depressed me for years because she didn't see a single thing in my future that I wanted to see. She insisted I would go into television, which was preposterous. I wasn't so gullible as to think she was right, I was just gullible enough to feel a shadow fall over me. I told her that her reading had ruined my peace of mind, and she laughed with great merriment.

Secondhand Rose

You put your hand on your shoulder and touch Carol's sweater, an intimate gesture given how angry you are. The sweater is one of several pieces of clothing she no longer wears and has given you, and several pairs of shoes she finds uncomfortable and has passed on. She has difficult feet and a weakness for shoes.

You are moving away and she has dropped you, casually, before you have moved. You are still here, but she isn't. The friend who said she could not imagine living in this city without you never calls.

You have thought of saying to her, Do you know how hurtful you are? Do you know how your casualness cuts into me? But you are too furious to do so.

And then when you become less furious – you are less furious now – you decide to use the same weapon of casualness against her. You will put on her shoes and walk over her with your casualness.

You can wear her almost-new shoes and say to yourself, They hurt her feet but they don't hurt mine. Look, she spent the money, but I've got them on. Hah!

Her black sweater has a hole you may mend, but you haven't mended it yet. It is a long loose sweater. You roll the sleeves above your elbows the way she used to (they roll up easily, the cuffs looser than they should be), and you see her arms, her face, her smile, and you feel lighthearted and immune. Today, after days of fury, you are in costume, part of the drama of two women leaving each other even as they merge: Carol has walked away leaving you with a bag of clothes, you are walking away wearing her, lightly, on your shoulders and feet. You even have her scarf around your neck. In wearing her clothes, you have assumed her elegance.

You get up to put on lipstick. It isn't yours or Carol's, but a stranger's. You found it in the change room at the swimming pool. *Lancôme. Champagne Rose.* It suits you perfectly.

You wear Carol's loose black sweater when you and your husband make love. Your arm moves around his back, you bend even lower, and in doing so smell the pool on your arm and think of *Champagne Rose* and the swimmer who can't wear it, because you have it.

There are moments when friends can be honest with each other about how wounded they feel, but you don't see a moment when this will happen. Those moments are never predictable anyway. They happen when you have given up hope of them ever happening, and come from a certain buoyancy in the air and in you, which makes it possible to speak of hurt in a sincere but lighthearted way.

You feel these other women on you – the lipstick kissed away, the sweater sliding off – and your husband holding you: holding three women at least in his arms.

Your husband says, "I would have to be pushed hard to believe anybody had dumped me."

"Why is that?" you ask.

"I guess it's my own defensiveness."

He means that he doesn't invite trouble. You see trouble everywhere, and defend yourself by exaggerating it and doing in the source.

Are you really engaged in a backhanded way of removing yourself from the picture? Are you busy imagining Carol's withdrawal in order to excuse, and secure, your own? Have you been manufacturing a small disaster in order to avoid a larger one? Feeling a small amount of pain acutely, hoping to avoid more? Who is trying to get away from whom? You are both, it seems, trying to get away from each other.

Carol says it's subconscious. "Because you're moving," she says. "I don't mean to pull away, but it's subconscious."

If it's subconscious, why is she talking about it?

This is the friend who criticized you months ago for not taking her birthday seriously enough, even though you took it much more seriously than she took yours. And haven't you been resentful about that ever since, along with other incidents you have never mentioned, allowing them to build up in your mind until they slide down and bury the friendship as if by natural and inexplicable causes?

You wonder how to make the predicament more interesting than friendship turning into drudgery. More interesting than Carol demanding a certain kind of attention that you provide, then you demanding a certain kind of attention she fails to provide.

It would be more interesting if you forgot about it. (You won't. Or you might until another incident reminds you and then the two incidents will proceed, lock-stepped, to trample over your mind.)

If you were to say, referring back to the birthday: Look. I cooked for you for three hours, I searched hard for a birthday present, I spent far more money than I normally spend, and what happens? In you walk and the first thing you say is, "I am so pissed off. It has to be on the day, my birthday has to be celebrated on the day."

If you could speak intently and dispassionately, getting the reaction you want: sheepishness, self-awareness. That would be interesting.

If you said, "You need more friends. If you had other friends, you wouldn't have been so disappointed when we couldn't celebrate on the day. Where are your other friends? Why do you have so few?"

But that would be mean. Besides, you know the answer. The friendships have ended in fights generated by that sort of question.

It is so predictable. From now on you will be on your guard against jumping to please even as you jump to please, and the friendship will leave the natural give and take of its early stages and enter the ritual of observances: her birthday must be observed, and in a particular way, or she will take offence. And only if you do not care about being scolded, only if you are deliberately casual and hold to your casualness as a point of honour, will you survive.

The exaggeration is part of the predictability. You have been through this many times, backing away from someone as touchy as yourself.

In the morning you stand rooted to the spot in front of the closet with several phrases repeating themselves in your head: *had you told us it mattered – I spent three, count them, three hours cooking – Who the hell are you, anyway?* – and staring at the clothing, a blur of mostly white, you feel utterly defeated. You will either express your opinion in a way that will backfire, or you will let it go. But it still isn't interesting because you still feel diminished.

Chewing on the same old bone. Get yourself a new one.

You rest your forehead against the cool white clothes and think that in some ways Carol is your closest friend, not in terms of time known but in the manner in which you have spent time together, and in her profession of friendship. She and Mario arrived in New York two years ago, lost and grateful souls whom you befriended. You were glad to do this because you liked them and because you were pleased to be in demand. They filled the hole Maureen once filled.

Now you watch them get used to your absence before you have even left. And while you never wholly believed their professions of friendship, still you wanted to believe them, and your desire to believe (which never slackens despite your scepticism which increases with every year), your desire to believe pains you. It pains you to be so vulnerable, and to be such a setpiece in Carol's display of adaptability.

Finally you stir yourself and dress. But all morning you snap at your children and your husband. He tells you not to get nervous, you tell him not to be so fucking patronizing.

You realize the next day, or perhaps the one after that, that his reaction to you when you first met is your reaction to Carol: He would be at his desk overlooking the park, he would turn to look at you as you talked on and on, he would turn away. You remember the order on his desk, and his coolness.

And yet you are still together.

There is something you haven't said. Your friends give you their old clothes because you never buy new ones. They know you will be happy with whatever they discard. This means that you are dressed in rejection and fatigue.

You are cheap in emotional ways too. If you were generous you would enjoy Carol for who she is. Instead, mean piece of Scottish shit that you are, you weigh the number of times she has called, the way people weigh out food in times of scarcity.

One of the pairs of shoes she passed along is made of soft expensive leather. Putting them on, you feel like a million dollars, less chafed by the world, better able to think the best rather than the worst. Yesterday a friend noticed them. He couldn't very well have missed. You stuck your foot under his nose and said, "Look!"

He asked where they came from and your answer was as natural and spontaneous as truth: "I am fortunate in my friends."

The Fight

A deep layer of snow has turned our broken-down Chevette into a dreamy Volvo. It hasn't moved for months and has never looked more beautiful. Carol and Mario used to borrow the car. This is part of the story – the car, and their borrowing.

I am wearing one of Carol's jackets. It doesn't have her smell any more, that expensive perfume whose name I can't remember. I used to open the closet and there it was, the ghost of my old friend who always went for men much younger than herself, spending money on them extravagantly, spending her attention more extravagantly still. The jacket is beautiful and beautifully made. Of all my friends, Carol had the best taste.

I'll begin with the borrowing. It happened one August and I remember the weather. It was a dark month during which light rain fell almost continuously. I turned on the lamp every morning and left it on all day. One morning I received a phone call which made me remember an earlier incident. I began to remember as I looked out the window at the rain, and by the time I stepped out the door the whole thing was running through my head. I crossed the street without looking, then walked towards the corner, the memory accelerated by the walking. I didn't think back to the phone call or my response: that he borrow the car in two hours because I was just leaving. I was already much farther along in my thoughts.

The air was mild. I opened my umbrella. At the corner I turned right, passing the fruit store, the liquor store, the shoe repair, the stationer's. A glimpse of yellow pen sets in the window, and the image of the light-green box camera, already in my mind, sprang forward with such force that it almost took my breath away. A large old-fashioned toy camera given to Ted when he was a child. He still has the photographs, small black-and-white shots of snow, trees, his backyard, fuzzy friends in the distance. I wonder if all children stand well back when they use a camera in the belief that exactly what they see will appear in the picture. I wonder when they realize that to make something come alive you have to choose an angle, correct the distance, exaggerate.

The camera was lost for a year. I remember putting it somewhere safe – a bunch of children were coming over, was it my daughter's birthday? – and I put it on a high shelf because I didn't want it broken. I did this with the camera and one or two other important toys. Also the baseball bat.

Over the course of the year my daughter asked for it repeatedly. I looked everywhere, several times, but never found it. Annie mentioned the loss to her grandmother who took the hint, but the new camera was smaller and poorly made; after an hour it was broken.

That was the year Carol, Mario and their kids were in Italy. When they got back Annie and I went over to see them. At one point the kids began to fight in the bedroom. I went to see why, and there was the camera. The two girls were sitting on a rug with a pile of toys between them, and on top of the pile was the camera. Could there be two?

"Where did it come from?" I asked them.

My five-year-old daughter said, "Emma stoled it from me."

The rain petered out and I lowered my umbrella. I bought a dozen oranges, then milk, chicken, and bread. I turned to go home and saw Carol's back fifty feet ahead of me: the long dark blue coat, red scarf, ankle-high soft leather boots. Her silver hair caught the light. I stopped in my tracks, then picked up my pace and caught up with her.

When I saw the old toy camera I picked it up and went into the kitchen. I said, "I've been looking for this for months."

Emma was on my heels and began to scream. Her whole small body took up the effort.

Carol said, "Oh dear. You see, she's just learned how to use it."

I was the one who apologized. "I'm sorry," I said over Emma's screams, "but Annie loves this camera too and has been asking for it for months."

"Oh dear," said Carol, and repeated, "You see, she just figured out how to use it." She bent down to comfort her daughter. "I'll buy one for her," she said. "Where do you get them?"

"It was given to Ted when he was a child. They don't make them any more."

"Oh. Well, that's even more . . ." and she didn't finish the sentence.

I couldn't pursue it. I reclaimed the camera, but I couldn't pursue it. In my head, however, I argued. Why didn't you give it back? Why didn't you ask if we wanted it back? Why did you assume that since it was important to your daughter, it was unimportant to mine? How could you?

In the street I caught up with her and we hugged each other.

These things coincide, genuine friendliness and genuine resentment, and for a while almost succeed in not colouring each other. Each seems pure – the friendliness, the resentment – undiluted and fresh. At a certain point the balance tips. Resentment washes over the friendliness and no attempt is made to see each other again unless one of the two friends persists, and then, with time, the balance tips the other way. Friendliness washes over the resentment, and you begin to believe the friendship has entered a new and wiser stage, and will endure.

"Ah, it's you," said Carol, smiling her deep real welcome. We walked to the end of the block, past the stretch of side-walk torn up in a different place each week and for no clear purpose. I had planned to go into the drugstore to get cough syrup for my daughter. I walked with Carol instead, as though breaking away to go into the store would be breaking away from the friendship.

At the corner Carol said they needed to borrow the car, they had to pick up a box of their belongings shipped from Italy.

I said yes, I knew. Mario had called.

There is so much balefulness under the surface of friendship. I wonder about it and give in to it, just as I often give in to the shy and savage impulse to cross the street and avoid someone I know. But I did not avoid Carol. We walked down the block together, genuinely glad to see each other, genuinely entering into the appearance of being glad. She invited us to come for dinner. "Saturday, Sunday, you pick," she said.

We kissed each other goodbye and I went home, lulled by her friendliness. I felt well-liked and this relaxed me.

2

Sunshine followed two days of rain. It was late September, the streets and air were clean, light filled any apartment higher than the second floor. Carol lived on the eleventh floor. She sat on her new sofa beside a row of windows and said she felt old.

"I am," she said, "I'm finally aging."

She had been aging for a long time: her hair had gone silver when she was thirty, she had had a child when she was forty, another when she was forty-two; fatigue had settled into her dark eyes and into her skin, but she was still very beautiful. She knew it and was attached to the idea: she wanted to be beautiful and to be reminded that she was. She also knew that hers was not a common beauty. Women appreciated her face far more than men.

The sofa was L-shaped and expensive, made of green fabric and light wood. I was sitting beside her and I said, "You look well."

"No. I don't."

"You do."

"Really?"

"Really."

She wasn't wearing makeup. She had stopped a few months ago, having worn it unfailingly for years. While not wanting to look old, she wanted to underscore her age. Mario was working in their bedroom down the hall. He was a student, fifteen years younger than she was, and the marriage was on the skids.

Before my arrival she had changed her T-shirt for a silk blouse and a necklace of silver and jade. She said to me, "I thought to myself, Beth is coming; let me put on one of my necklaces."

I watched her with a certain tenderness not because she wasn't as beautiful any more, and she wasn't, but because she could have been had she been less troubled by her age. I enjoyed her face the way Mario should have. Carol knew this, it was almost an unstated joke between us. We sat together on the sofa, saying what a relief it was to look at things that were pleasing to the eye, and we knew we were talking not just about the sofa, but about each other. She told me not to cut my hair and never to get bangs. "I've never liked bangs," she said. "Women with strong faces shouldn't wear bangs." (I'm wearing bangs now, several years later, and she's right. It was a mistake.)

Then she showed me photographs of Mario. Look at him, she said, just look at him: he could be a movie star. They were pictures of the birth of the second child: Mario held the baby in front of the hospital window, then Carol held the baby in front of the same window, he as unaffected by the birth as she had been changed – her face wide, white, and exhausted. She didn't want to be a young man's old wife, but she had let herself fall in love and now she was letting herself look old. These lapses in her resistance – falling in love, getting old – were at the same time displays of resistance: to being old, to being unloved.

I sat with my back twisted slightly to the side so that I faced her. Even though the position was uncomfortable and my back began to hurt I didn't move, because any shift might have led Carol to believe that I wasn't as interested as I appeared to be. I struck a pose for fixed friendship. I was a statue with rocks in my head. A woman with no notion, not so much as the N of a notion, of how to move easily and as myself inside a friendship. So of course the friendship had to fail, and probably as explosively as it did.

The new sofa was an investment in their marriage. Carol and Mario stood in the store and he said, "Buy it."

"But the price!"

"Buy it."

Mario studied out of sight and hearing down the hall, his shoulders bent over his books. He was far behind Carol in most ways: she dominated with her experience, her education, her command of the language, her money. But an older woman's pride is nothing compared to a young man's physical vanity and lack of self-reproach. Before the birth, on the day Carol was expecting to go into labour, she sat at my kitchen table and tried to get Mario to pay attention to her. He only had eyes for my two-year-old son with whom he played.

"I get very childish at times like this," she said. "I start to say, I don't want to be here." By *here* she meant the hospital. "I don't want to be here." And she talked about getting an epidural as soon as she went in.

I told her to be sure to take food along. I had given birth at three in the morning, not eaten until eight, and suffered from hypoglycemia all the next day. She said to Mario, "Listen. You should be listening to this." But he was all smiles, all don't worrys, all pleasantness, absence, evasion, putdown. Playing with my little boy.

"I'll be surrounded by women," he told me after learning the second child would be a girl.

"Are you disappointed?"

"Oh no. I adore women."

I told Carol that she looked great. "Doesn't she look beautiful," I said to Mario.

He looked away, off into space, and after a moment he said, "Sometimes."

I had attention to offer. I focused on Carol, was expected to focus on her, because her husband did not. Had the marriage been different, the friendship would have been different, not in its mechanics but in the intensity of its tone and the quality of its relief. Carol welcomed me like a new and peaceful landscape.

In October she insisted she was all right, even while tears welled up in her eyes and her face constricted and changed colour. We sat for an hour and a half in a restaurant, Carol playing with the utensils she didn't use and saying little, me playing with the dead skin on my elbows and saying less. She didn't want to talk about the marriage. Had never wanted to talk about it in detail. She would say, "It's awful, just awful." I would ask why and she would answer, "It's so awful I can't talk about it."

She liked to state things in extremes. Something was *terrible*. Something else was *awful*. That must be *awful* for you, she would say, and you would think no, it's not so awful, but feel pleased she thought so, as though she had handed you a compliment. She dominated the conversation not with talk, but with her pauses which I didn't know how to fill, with her tears which she wiped away, and her reassurances that she was fine. She liked the drama of announcing something without explaining it. And so her mood dominated, her problems dominated, her thoughts dominated, but they did not satisfy.

Our small square table had two paper napkins and two sets of utensils provided by the hopeful waiter, one glass of red wine, and one beer and a glass. Carol drank her beer quickly, I drank my wine slowly. It was the wrong wine. I had asked for white.

"Will it be wasted if you take it back?" I asked the waiter. Yes, it would be thrown out. "Then I'll drink it."

Carol didn't understand this. "You ordered white," she said, "you wanted white."

The restaurant was large, well-used, and on a corner, an easy place to meet. I used to come here, I told her, with two other friends who were taking the same film course. I was thinking that it was easier to come with two people than with one. The thought didn't articulate itself except as an overeager smile.

It smelled of Paris to Carol. She said so out loud. "It smells of Paris," sniffing the coffee in the air. This should have been a pleasant association but it wasn't; her sister had just died in Paris, she had gone to the funeral and found the city too polished, too full of tourists. A place you pass through, a restaurant you pass through – a friendship – with the same attitude as a traveller's: curious, uncommitted, detached.

"It's so tough on Emma," she finally said.

"It's tough on you too," I said.

She smiled through her tears and repeated that it was tough on her daughter.

I wanted to know what would happen, where Mario would go if they split up, how she would manage with a small child and a baby, whether she regretted having the baby, whether she blamed herself. But none of the questions seemed appropriate either because they were too personal, or because they were unanswerable.

I reached across the table and took her small hand. First I touched the little finger the way you might a child's curled-up fist, to make it open. Her fingers loosened, gave way, and pressed mine in turn. She smiled again and wiped her eyes. Then she started to talk about her past. She had always fallen for men much younger or much less educated than herself, creating a new imbalance in order to right the age-old imbalance between men and women. A recipe for failure and something that didn't bear examination, the failing of a marriage no one thought would work.

And the failing now of friendship. She was quick to finish her beer, quick to realize the visit wasn't satisfying and wouldn't be, quick to feel bored and want to get away. But I was slow with my wine, intent upon finding some way to show my affection and desire to help, even as I had no help to offer and nothing to say.

3

In an old notebook I find the beginning of my first fight with Carol and the beginning is so peaceful. We were on a ferry at midnight, the sea breezes soft and cool, the kids asleep in the back seat of the old Chevette. We leaned against the railing, Ted and I, our bodies still hot from the city and stiff from the car, and felt a brief, quick sense of voyage. We came to an island full of deep green hollows in one of which we found Carol's cottage lit up like something Japanese made of paper and wood.

I come upon this scene by chance and feel the sudden dread, the sense of inevitability, about what is coming next. We had known Carol and Mario, at this point, for six months. That night we slept in their cottage, the next day we swam in a pond. Carol said, "It's amazing to be surrounded by salt water and swimming in a freshwater pond." The day after that we were having our first salty-corrosive spat in the middle of a soft afternoon. I had just criticized her for her overwrought *ohs* of lament whenever her daughter Emma got upset.

"You mean her traumas aren't really traumas?" acidly. "They're not as real as adult traumas?"

I was irked because the day before Carol had spoken sharply to my daughter. Her remarks had occurred on the beach and were hardly severe. "Annie, it's not that impor-tant," when Emma attacked and spilled her pie plate of sand, Annie crying out as Emma hit it. Then Annie said something was hers which wasn't. Carol said, "No. It's *not* yours."

But when Emma spilled her own pie plate of sand it was, "Poor Emma! Oh, *poor* Emma!"

Mothers who think their children can do no wrong went the bitter little chant in my head. I expect this is fairly common. Women often meet each other as mothers, in playgrounds, outside stores, on the beach, drawn together by mutual need, only to discover in a few days, or weeks, or months, that as mothers we can't stand each other. Later that same day I yelled fiercely at Annie twice. Then I brooded about my behaviour, suspecting that my harshness with Annie gave others the licence to be harsh, and knowing that my harsh-ness was a reflection of my tension about her as a child and about myself as a mother. No mystery here, just the usual unbearable nature of family life. But it laid the groundwork for my impulsive criticism of Carol the following day.

She cooked bacon as we fought, burning it on too hot a stove, then she dumped the frypan into the sink and scoured furiously while I poked at my eyes with an orange towel.

Dissecting the fight now, I remember the incredibly beautiful light-green praying mantis we found on a leaf exactly the same shade. Carol had been looking for the source of a certain fragrance and had found it in a high lush hedge yards away from the sea. On one of the leaves she found the praying mantis. She said, "I think I'll come back here tonight to sleep."

That beautiful bug, invisible in its beauty, having become the leaf. While I stood out. Made myself stand out. Pushed myself into the open and got creamed.

Carol: you aren't honest; your comments are under-handed; if you were upset with me, why didn't you just say so?

Me: conversations aren't always perfectly staged, we say things impulsively; I'm out of sorts; maybe, I said patheti-cally, I'm pregnant.

And what I thought and didn't say: I am afraid of you. No matter what I said you would have taken it as criticism, and attacked, and won.

I was so full of tears (people who cry easily should never fight) that I had to leave the house. I walked out through the sliding glass door, leaving Ted and Mario with their softly dismayed faces hovering over the children, and across the lawn and down the road to the sea. I was a child again. I was too small for the big mess I had made. I was walking down a dusty road in the full heat of midday, quivering in shock from the head-on collision I had just staged. I couldn't believe that I had created something so punishing for myself and so full of reverberations for everyone else. For half an hour I walked. Then I went back.

I came across the lawn and beautiful Carol dressed in pink spread out her arms and welcomed me back. I almost went down on my knees in gratitude.

One year went by, and I was careful. Carol and Mario went to Italy the next year. They came back and seven more careful months went by. Then we had our big fight.

I began to write about the fight this morning, safe in my little room in Ottawa, when the phone rang. Carol was calling from New York. We had not spoken in two years, and she was calling. Such is the magnetism of stories and guilt. I listened to her voice, feeling horror, affection, and the old desire to make myself likeable. She needed something from Ted and I would give him the message; it was wonderful to hear each other's voices; we would do our utmost to get together, and so on. I hung up and wrote down the words: Nothing escapes her. I wrote down: I am taken over by what I'm drawn to: her vivid, effusive, perceptive, exaggerating presence. I wrote: I am afraid she will read this, yet I write it anyway; always afraid of someone's reaction, yet writing anyway. I feel her glittering eyes cutting into me, seeing all there is to see.

Then I went back to the story the way you seek refuge in an open hiding place, fully exposed yet somewhat comforted; a child under a table, surprised that others can see her when she can't see them, yet never able to come up with a better spot.

In the story it was November and Emma was having a birthday. Carol had invited a dozen children and their parents for a Saturday afternoon party. At the party the kids tore across the living-room floor while we parents sat in a row against the wall. Each time the bell rang Carol went down the long curving hallway to open the door. I was too busy wondering where Mario was to offer to help, until she asked me to. "Beth," she said, "the next time the bell rings, could you?"

So Beth walked down the hallway and in passing their bedroom poked her curious head inside. He was there, the movie star bent over his books. He looked up and smiled at his wife's friend, managing to grimace at the pile of papers on his desk even as he smiled. I was his stand-in. The substitute husband.

After my first spat with Carol, Ted said to me, re-creating the moment in the cottage, "I thought, she's not really going to say this, and then you said it." He spoke with almost clinical kindness. He didn't condemn me. He seizes the high road always, and without effort.

He and Carol are still very good friends. He sees her whenever he goes to New York and reports back. She is well, she looks well, extremely well, wonderful, he says. Everything is going well, extremely well. She sends you lots and lots of love.

Does he think I want to hear this? No, probably not. He thinks I *should* hear it. I am glad when he tells me these things in bed, with the lights out, because then I can make all sorts of faces without his seeing.

The first spat laid the groundwork for the big fight. It made me careful, it made me quiet; it made me all the things I am naturally, but more so. After Carol forgave me at the cottage, after we returned to the city and as soon as they returned two weeks later, I called her. I wanted to prove that

I could be a good and lasting friend. There is a sort of innocence in me that my darkness rescues me from, but for what?
I am never sure.

Emma had her birthday in November, Carol had her birthday in December (the one that should have been celebrated
on the day), and in January Carol and Mario went alone to
Venice for a two-week holiday. In that dreamy setting they
fell in love again. They came home happy, and their happiness spoiled mine. For the next few months I saw very little
of them and I got increasingly angry.

My anger came on early in the morning like a tidal wave,
astonishing me with its size. I would lean against the kitchen
counter and hang on. In my mind Carol would make some
small comment – a sneer – a criticism – and I would explode
back with such derision, viciousness, and pent-up hatred that
it rocked me. After all, I was fond of Carol. I remembered
that I was fond and then I tried to remember why.

My mood swung around my head like a rope with a stone
at the end – something I had seen illustrated in a book – a
man swinging it, then letting it go to tangle around a bird on
the wing. In Argentina they use these things to prevent birds
from landing, swinging them far and wide over the pampas
until the birds die of exhaustion. But how can enough people
swing enough *bolas*, that's the word, to keep the birds from
coming to rest on distant grass? I drank my cold coffee (in
my anger I had forgotten making it), then on impulse I called
Carol. She was glad to hear from me and we laughed, we
joked, we arranged to see each other; she said she had some

clothes she wanted to pass along, I said wonderful. Even I found this breathtaking. It was as if my anger had never existed. But it did exist. It had lit on a farther field to rest.

In the evening I prepared dinner and my shoulders got harder and harder. My body was turning to concrete. It occurred to me that much of my anger came from fear. I was afraid that Carol had turned against me. Almost immediately I felt suspicious of this thought. How could anyone walk five paces from the counter to the phone to talk to the very person she had been raging at as though they were the best of friends? The hypocrisy shocked me. Yet I wasn't willing to say that my affection for Carol was hypocritical.

I thought, I only get this angry with someone I really love. The anger is a sign of love.

Then I felt suspicious of that thought too. First, because I was angry with everyone under the sun. Second, because I felt no love whatsoever.

Months before we had promised to spend Passover together. In early April I called her to make plans. She didn't call back for several days. When she did, we discussed the meal. Then she said, "Are you angry at me?"

I paused. "Yes," I said. "I'm annoyed."

"Can you say another sentence?"

"It's a long story," I said. And then, "Well, it's not such a long story."

And briefly I explained the components of my sense of rejection, which formed a short story that had occurred so often it was a long story. I tried to find words for my feelings without seeming to be a complete fool, since all of this certainly had its foolish aspect, and I managed to say that she and Mario rarely called any more: we had had a certain kind of friendship, it had changed a great deal, I felt angry and hurt.

Carol was patient, even graceful. She accepted what I was saying, even saying that I was right, but somehow the conversation didn't know where to go. I didn't say: Oh, everything is all right then, I'm sorry for thinking the worst of you. She didn't say: Well, let's try harder to see each other without appearing to try harder. The conversation petered out and I had to think of an excuse to hang up.

The following Thursday, at two-thirty in the afternoon, the phone rang. I went into the kitchen and picked up the light grey phone off its small blue shelf. I stood while Carol talked.

She said our conversation had been bothering her. She said that my anger and hurt were unjustified. She had been sick and I could have been more attentive, our encounters had been fewer but their quality had remained unchanged. She said I had ten times the social life she had anyway and why hadn't I taken up any complaints I had about Mario with Mario himself.

"Why not?" she asked. "Why haven't you called him?"

I felt the old old sensation. The one where your insides give way and slop around like water.

She went on. "You are really pulling a number. You think you're the only person bad things happen to."

"*Bullshit*," I said, anger suddenly coming to my rescue.

"You're like Rosana," a former friend of hers she often complained about. "You're into this thing of wanting to feel victimized, you're always –"

But I cut her off. I yelled, "THAT'S BULLSHIT! " And I hung up.

I had imagined that fight for weeks, and finally it happened. I had imagined hanging up on Carol, and I hung up on her. The next morning I felt as if a huge weight had been lifted off every part of me. We had written each other off. It was mutual. Even. Over. I lay in bed, peaceful and refreshed.

The next day I felt less buoyant.

The day after that Ted told me he had bumped into Carol in the street. She had told him she felt terrible and thought she understood what had happened. He said he didn't want to know what had happened, he just hoped we would resolve it.

But she didn't call and I didn't call. I got up from my desk at work and my stomach ached. I imagined meeting her. I imagined saying, "excuse me," and leaving.

We used to dress for each other, not conspicuously but consciously. We noticed each other and were glad to be noticed. The pleasure of looking and being looked at generated serenity rather than sex: the days of sexual romance are over, I thought to my nearly forty-year-old self, the romance of friendship has begun.

We were both fascinated by the way women age. We would walk down the street looking at women in their fifties, following with our eyes the ones with sufficient means to weather life with style and grace. We admired and envied them.

One evening we went to a piano recital in a museum, entering through the back door and taking a carpeted hallway to the auditorium. A woman in blue waited beside the door. She was fifty-five, perhaps sixty, and in the company of another woman and a man of about the same age. Her white hair was fashioned into a bun at the nape of her neck, she had finely wrinkled skin, red lipstick, terrific posture, gold earrings in the shape of shells. We stopped a few feet away from her and waited until it was time to go in. Our glances shifted around, but always returned to the woman in blue.

We followed her into the concert hall, taking seats behind her and to the side, drawn to her, relaxed by the sight of her. Isn't she beautiful, we murmured to each other. During the concert our eyes shifted back and forth between the small bald twinkling pianist on stage and the woman's straight shoulders, jaw, neckline, hair. We studied her: a painting, a room, another way of life.

In Carol I had found a similar pleasure: someone to observe and contemplate: a view. For a while our friendship was almost cinematic.

The aftermath was a surprise. Three weeks after our fight Carol invited us for lunch. She greeted me with a hug and said she had missed me. There were no traces of the fight except, it seemed, in me. She called me Bethie.

It was a Sunday afternoon and raining. We had planned to go to the park and were in her apartment instead.

We had never discussed our fight. We had referred to it when we made contact two weeks after it happened, but only to say – I said, I made the call – that I hadn't called sooner because I was afraid of getting into another fight. And we alluded to it when we discussed qualities our children possessed – bad temper, fatigue, an inability to communicate – explaining without apologizing (neither of us apologized) our own behaviour. The burden of these conversations in which we couldn't speak directly weighed on me, and yet I didn't trust Carol enough to change the way I spoke – Carol of the razor-sharp tongue and rapid-fire assumptions.

It was half a friendship the way you have half a marriage or half a life. You might think there would be no need to have this kind of friendship, yet I have had many.

She had invited another couple, so there were six adults around the table and various children darting from room to room. We stayed for several hours. As soon as we got home, the phone rang. It was Carol. "I feel bad," she said. "We barely saw each other all afternoon. We should get together by ourselves."

I smiled. "We saw each other."

"But we didn't get a chance to really talk."

We had talked as much as we wanted to. But I went along with her suggestion that we get together.

"Or," she said, "we could get a babysitter for our children and the four of us could go out for dinner, as adults."

Clearly we were relieved by this alternative.

And yet she had been so transparently friendly all afternoon that I wondered about myself. I felt milky with the past, an unexpressed past to which I kept returning in my

head but not out loud. Was mine sadness at the loss of
friendship? Or sadness at my inability to be a friend? Or
sadness at my inability to end a friendship in a friendly way?

There were several lush new plants in her apartment. I
touched the fern, gently turning over a leaf, and was delighted
to see rows of white specks, and upon closer inspection,
cobwebs, small and delicate. I wondered if there was any
limit to my pettiness.

The paintings were in different places. I looked at them
as though for the first time. "Was this here before? Is this
new?" Nothing was new, but everything had shifted. I hadn't
been in the apartment for several months.

At the table they were saying the only constant is change,
everything is always changing. I said no, certain things
remain steady. In my mind I saw salmon, gigantic turtles, and
myself, refusing to learn from experience and throwing ourselves against the same old dam, plopping down on the same
old beach, returning to the same old wound – the scene
where friendship is born and goes wrong – to this apartment
which a wiser person would have avoided.

Carol and I could not say: Look at us. Look at us avoiding each other while pretending we're not. The most we
could do was remain in contact without seeming to overdo
the contact, and cushion the contact with other people.

I wondered how long this would last.

◆

They have been fighting, and though they're not fighting
now, you can hear the earlier fight in their voices. They're

talking on the phone because they are afraid to see each other. They are talking cautiously but one of them has more confidence, more breeziness in her manner, and she is talking less. The one who is less sure of herself is talking more, and this annoys her: once again she is at a disadvantage.

During the fight the uncertain one said too much. She should never have begun the discussion (forgetting that she didn't begin it), and once she found herself in it, should have found a way out, short of yelling bullshit and hanging up.

They are talking. They have nothing to say to each other, but they are talking so the friendship won't seem to end the way it did, but be given a peaceable burial. Neither of them believes they will see each other much after this call. From time to time, but not much. Not the way they used to.

It is four in the afternoon, an hour later than the phone call several weeks earlier that ended so explosively.

The one who is uncertain detects some amusement, wryness, in the other's tone. Her own questions seem artificial. They skirt the disaster and hang up.

It won't be easy. They will convey with their questions and tones of voice the trappings of friendship, but the effect will be hollow and strange, so that while they speak they will want to stop speaking, but they'll keep on, because there is no natural ending to what has ended unnaturally.

Cowgirl

Beth thought of herself – this was after putting on Carol's brown leather boots – as a cowgirl with notches in her belt for friendships wrestled to the ground and hauled off for slaughter. Plenty of slaughter and all in her mind. Not for the first time she envied the more active life of men and their peaceable if almost non-existent friendships. Few of the men she knew had many friends.

A cowgirl shooting down Indians, wrestling actively and all the time with unfriendly cattle, sleeping under an open sky which meant not sleeping much. Counting up notches in her belt.

But no physical release. The Wild West was bottled up in her brain, racketing around up there until she was tired, lassoed, worked over and tied up by her own thoughts.

Beth got back from the meeting after ten, too dismayed to talk. Ted followed her into the kitchen where she made a face and gestured with her hands to indicate: mess.

"Something went wrong?" he asked.

And still she couldn't talk. But finally she said something. She explained what happened.

"That leak from Anabel's apartment has been going on for months. Henry showed us the damage and I said we have to say who's responsible. If your apartment is the source of the leak you have to fix it, you have to act. And Anabel got huffy and said I was blaming her, I was always making a fight, and she was leaving. I said, 'No. You *can't* leave. You have to stay. I'll leave.' And I left."

"Good for you," said Ted.

Beth said, "Well – it's all awkward now."

"Well, maybe it has to be," he said.

That made her feel better. She hadn't said she was a schmuck, he hadn't said she was a schmuck. However, she still felt like a schmuck.

Her mother had always complained about her tone of voice. "Why are you so belligerent?" her mother would ask. It had never seemed like much of a question. Her mother made her angry, so did her father and one of her brothers. It was only a good question now because it had been going on for so long. Ted believed she liked to be angry. He went so far as to say she needed to be angry. "I don't understand," he said, "your need for anger."

Beth walked past Anabel, out the door and down the hall, and heard Anabel say, "She's always like that," while someone else said, "May I make a suggestion?" And what she felt as she walked down the hall, besides relief at getting away, was a sort of sick dismay. Things had gone wrong and once again she was to blame. Her temper was to blame.

She had fought with Anabel before. Anabel hadn't paid her rent for the two years she had been president of the co-op, and it had taken long hours of bookkeeping and a lot of arm-twisting to get her to begin to pay her arrears. It had fallen to Beth to do the arm-twisting.

Anabel is a big woman. Beth sees her in the street in her padded yellow jacket with her large head of hair, and she doesn't flee. She smiles weakly and says hello. Anabel smiles too, even though they can't stand each other. There has been a leak from her bathroom to the bathroom below, and sometimes the one below that, for six months. The people below find it easier to come to Beth than to deal with Anabel.

Beth lies in bed reading a story about a woman who is virtually immobilized except for her anger. She wonders if this is the main female fuel – anger – and if so, why.

She remembers Anabel's face as the discussion about the leak began, the deliberately blank look that came over her – a woman who hopes that if she does nothing the building will do everything – and her quick accusation that Beth was blaming her, her quick move to remove herself, which Beth countered handily, she has to admit, in the process leaving everyone else to clean up her mess.

She can't sleep. Whenever she has a fight with someone she can't sleep.

What is going through her head? The fight, of course. Every detail, everything that anyone said, and future fights. She is awake to the future and to questions about her character. She tries hard not to care what people think of her, but she still must care a great deal because as she lies awake she feels that a spotlight is trained on her: she is exposed, as herself, for everyone to see.

She walked down the hallway in the blue corduroy pants and brown leather boots passed along by Carol (with whom she fought two weeks ago) while she heard Anabel say, "She's always like that."

What she really wants to do is sock somebody in the kisser. Men get to sock each other in the kisser and it must make them feel a lot better.

She wants to lasso real cattle on a real plain, then hunker down beside a fire and brew a nasty cup of coffee. Maybe a dog for company, maybe a bottle or two of gin.

A Personal Letter

Strange how we become different with different people. I write to you and feel myself being reshaped, not saying certain things, saying other things, always with you in mind. If I were writing to Susan, how different this letter would be. You never met her, but the two of you knew people in common.

I've been reading Thurber. At the moment I like him more than E. B. White. He has more animosity. White is sweetly wise: the decent, honest, understated American writing at thirty as if he were sixty. With Thurber you can see the wounds, the rumpled clothes, the short-sighted blinking stare. I've been reading his description of Scott Fitzgerald and Zelda: ". . . rarely relaxed enough for true comedy or comfortable enough for genuine humour, they seemed to move dramatically, from the beginning, in settings designed for tragedy."

Thurber is much more bitter than White (at least in these posthumous essays) and I like his bitterness – his anger – for itself, and for the tenderness and generosity that shoot through it. He appears to have been a wonderful friend, though writers tend to be better friends on paper than in person. He and White were wonderful friends until they had a falling out over some inexcusable rudeness of Thurber's, I think. Some transgression.

You introduced me to White. Do you remember? You mentioned how fine his writing was, and I went to the beautiful old library beside the river and couldn't believe how good his essays were. You were my well-read friend.

That was a long time ago. I remember your very white skin and the set of your mouth. I didn't realize how unhappy you were, or how funny, or how down-to-earth. The combination of mouth, skin, and glasses – large glasses, tight mouth – threw me off. I had no idea then of the rejection you were living through and still are. A man saw you in a particular light and after he left the light stayed on.

You told me I was very serious. We were down in the cafeteria drinking coffee and it was a summation of my character. We had known each other less than a year, and I'd been so proud of how I had made you laugh.

This is the tragedy of love. We are most serious with the people we most admire, and the people we most admire love to laugh.

You say my letters are funny. That's because when I'm feeling funny I tend to write to you. I have to be in a particular mood – friendly, forgiving, companionable – since you almost never write back. Often the best letters occur when I don't feel like writing but write anyway. I say whatever enters my head, unworried until after the letter is mailed.

There was a period when I couldn't write to you at all. I had written twice, you hadn't answered; I had visited (seeing Stephen in the hospital) and become convinced you thought poorly of me. This went on for a year. Then I called you from the airport, passing through, a two-hour wait, a phone call I almost didn't make, and you were so pleased to hear from me and we talked so easily that I wondered what all the fuss had been about.

Thurber and Fitzgerald met only once. They didn't feel the need to stay in touch. Maybe that's what a good friend is: not someone with a long attention span, not someone who stays in touch, but someone who refuses to take us all that seriously, then writes about us in a flattering way. Thurber wrote his essay and it was really a portrait of loyalty: Fitzgerald to Zelda, Fitzgerald to Hemingway, Fitzgerald to Ring Lardner, Thurber to Fitzgerald.

You taught me about loyalty. You were the one who put flesh on that bone. You said, "The most wounding and terrifying thing about T is that he's incapable of loyalty."

So why don't you write to me?

You'll need my new address. I've been packing all week. Around my desk are boxes of books and a black garbage bag full of old papers. I've been going through old writing, appalled at how many versions of the same lousy piece I've kept. Again and again I find a small interesting observation passed over in favour of a "telling" image or metaphor. I'm always trying to make what I see *into* something, in an odd and unhappy overextension of myself.

There is something I want to say. Or perhaps to confess. It has to do with the time I went to see Stephen. I found him on the fifth floor in a private room, an altogether different man: serene, open, at peace with himself. "It's a relief," he told me. "David has it and I wouldn't want to be alive if he isn't."

I came back to your house and you said, "It must be so painful for you. It must be just awful."

I shook my head and didn't answer. Then I said it should be more awful than it is. You looked at me and said you didn't believe that.

You would have cared more. I picture you hearing the news, then drawing the curtains and lying down for several hours. In my mind your hands are over your face, and your face is pressed against the back of the dark red sofa.

You met David only once. We went over to his apartment and had supper together. It was early summer and warm, long before (or maybe not so long before) he got sick. We sat on the balcony as he set food on the granite slab he used as a tabletop. An unmarked gravestone he had dragged home from somewhere. You may have been the one to notice that.

You talked about your daughter. Have I ever told you how your voice changes when you speak to her? How tender it becomes? David was teaching art to children and you asked him many questions about creativity. You were very precise in your questions, and he was vague in his answers. You liked each other.

Now I think of you and David in the same breath.

I should have written to him more often. Months went by between the letters I sent, and they were cards as often as letters. I suppose it was hard to write because of my phoniness. I wrote the letters (the cards) knowing how much he wanted to come for a visit, but never inviting him despite my expressions of love. I was afraid of having to explain to Frank the landlord what sort of sickness he had as I shouldered him up and down the stairs.

2

Sweet of you to call (I say this and hear Claude Rains saying to Ingrid Bergman, "Sweet of you to wait." If you knew how many times I've watched *Notorious* you'd lock me up.) Since we spoke I've been sitting here thinking, as I often do, about the sort of friendship that lasts. I've been home long enough to see which New York friendships have fallen away, and which old friendships in Canada have remained. I usually conclude that the amount of room we give each other is the key. *Room* and *generosity* are the words that float around in my mind. But I like your word better. *Consistency.* You were saying you don't register with your students because you are always the same, while other teachers, more mercurial, vivid, unpredictable, even mean, carry children along in their wake. You said children don't appreciate what we come to value so much as adults: consistency in our relationships.

Some old hurt was in your voice, along with mild outrage and your usual eloquence, as you described the teacher with perfect hair who shakes her wave effortlessly into place a hundred times a day.

It's late. I hear the cars on the highway and think of you listening. This is an old woman's pleasure, and a child's. Last night Annie called out at three in the morning, her eyes wide with nightmare, and we listened to the cars for quite a while. Was it your sister who was so devastated when Glenn Gould died, leaving her without the certainty that at least one other person in Toronto was also awake?

I see you with the bedside light on, a book in your hands. You are still my well-read friend. I hesitate to say this, too superstitious to put good things into words, but I say it anyway. What would I do without you?

Sayonara

I saw him in the library. I was coming upstairs from the lower level devoted to fiction to the main level check-out. He was at the counter, in profile, old and composed. His skin was smooth, his hair was evenly grey, he was wearing an elegant black coat. This was the first time I had seen him in eight years.

I hesitated for only a second (Peter eyeing Mr. McGregor and beyond him the gate), then walked quickly right behind him, my eyes fixed on the turnstile ahead, and beyond that, the revolving doors. Whether he saw me when I passed behind him or recognized me from the back (I would have recognized him from any angle), I don't know. I passed within two feet of him and had to wait for a man to emerge from the revolving doors. Then the doors spat me into the lobby where sliding doors opened and I was in the street.

Still I didn't relax. I stood on the corner with my back to the library straddling both possibilities: left or right, whichever first turned green, waiting to spring forward at the first break in traffic. For the rest of the day I felt shaken, overpowered by the black and dapper figure waiting to check out books.

The new black coat was a surprise. Could it be cashmere? Leonard Brooks in a cashmere coat? But that would require money and he didn't spend money. Leonard the non-spender, Leonard the non-reader, Leonard alone – who was never alone. In an expensive new coat and unaccompanied, taking out books.

At home I made a pot of tea and looked out the window for a long time. I looked for big words to balance all the hurts – innocence, betrayal, humiliation. But big words don't begin to compensate for small memories: the film of grime in his bathroom, the smell from the one damp towel, the stray hairs in the sink and on the floor, the tired joke about his new pair of sheets waiting for the right occasion, the thought of his body, his softness, his sentimentality. The pity he aroused, the companionship he offered, the need he sensed in me, the need he cultivated so well. The cardboard box he used for a bedside table, the late-night phone calls, the unannounced arrivals for dinner, the refusal to buy furniture, the man as child, the sexual fear. He used to phone me after I had fallen asleep and say, "Meet me for breakfast at the Star Café, eight o'clock, don't be late. And Bethie?"

"Yes."

"We're making memories."

Here are some memories, Bethie's memories of Leonard B.

Soft waist. Receding hairline. Long nails. The kindness and manipulation. The propriety and dishonesty. The cagey unconscious bullshit.

I remember him telling me once, when he was very tired, that he felt like a crushed rose. It was evening. He was sitting across from me in a booth in a restaurant, a small prematurely old man resting his head in his left hand, the palm scarred from breaking a lamp when he was three, the slender fingers tipped by those unnerving nails.

"When you were growing up what did you want to be?" I asked him.

"A child," he said. "I was happy as a child."

The child rarely strayed from the movies on TV. He absorbed Maurice Chevalier's smile, too large for a face that retained the pallor and quickness-to-tire of a long boyhood sickness. His eyes were permanently soft and tender, tattooed by the pale blue light from so much secondhand romance. "You have to see *Moulin Rouge*," he told me, "it teaches so much about loneliness."

I had heard this before. I didn't think I had much to learn about loneliness. By this time, Leonard made me feel lonelier than anyone else I knew.

There was the man's growth of hair on those soft boy arms, uncultivated, unwanted, unweeded, like long hairs dangling from the sides of a brush, or pubic hairs gone grey and sparse. There was the way he put his arms around my waist and pulled me towards his face. I would smile, turn my head to one side, or lean back if our foreheads touched. Those hugs went on for a long time, each one and all of them together, pressing me against his soft body while he whispered into my ear, "Mad about you, so mad about you." I turned my head away from his breath.

We used to work together and we used to work late (I mean *late*; sometimes finishing the magazine at dawn), then we walked through Allan Gardens past the illuminated fountain, the greenhouse, the flowerbeds, to a bench where we sank down and breathed in the heavy scent of dust, fumes, grass, garbage, perfume. Leonard talked and I listened. Politics, old movies, baseball, odd encounters, figures from history; he had a way with an anecdote, a joke, a telling phrase; I listened, and there wasn't a single thing he said that wasn't interesting. What do I remember now of all those well-turned sentences? That he loved Johnny Carson, that he wanted to be on TV, that he saw himself as a natural entertainer, a witty unassuming moral figure who deserved uninterrupted applause.

He was thirty-five and seemed older. I was twenty-seven and seemed younger. Younger and nicer.

He walked me to the streetcar, then wouldn't let me get on. Just one more block. Then another. All the way to Parliament Street.

His hands tightened if I pulled away too soon. Shapely hands with single long hairs growing out of the soft skin on their backs. In elementary school a girl had told him he had nice fingernails for a boy.

In the beginning I felt sure of my footing. I didn't take his whispers seriously and enjoyed his company – he was unaffected, knowledgeable, and kind – and I felt chosen, honoured in a way, to receive so much attention. And then the friendship turned. There must have been a moment, if I can only think hard enough, when I turned from a listening, flattered, indulgent friend into an insecure worker, humiliated in some indefinable way but so thoroughly that I felt myself crack. I can think of a certain moment.

It was nearly midnight and everyone else had gone home. Leonard came over to my desk with his coat on. His small round face was tired and in need of a shave, but he looked keyed-up and strangely intent.

"You have to go?" I said.

"Yes," he said. "And you have to come with me." His words were firm and deliberate. I think he had practised that line.

"*Casablanca*," I said, and his face fell.

"Damn Richard." Richard had taped a note to the cafeteria wall saying the movie would be on at midnight.

I stood up. Leonard hugged me and I pulled back, careful to do so gradually, but he saw the look on my face.

"It wasn't to be a test," he said, nervous, apologetic, giddy. "Just a little game."

The little game: pretending to take me home to his bed.

Outside it was dark and cool. We walked under leafy trees beside large old houses that were very quiet, but not as quiet as we were. The only word in my head was *tired*. In his apartment I sat on the sofa, he took the armchair and murmured much of the dialogue: "Maybe not today, maybe not tomorrow, but soon and for the rest of your life."

Not long afterwards I dreamt that I was being led into a motel by Leonard. His name was on the register and above it were the names of prostitutes he had brought before. I tried to run away, but the air pulled at my knees so that I barely moved. Then I was walking down the road. Headlights appeared and to my enormous relief it was X, the man I was in love with. He pulled up beside me in his old car. He got out and spoke to me. I think he smiled as he motioned with his head towards the motel. He was trying to get me to go back. I went back.

Leonard's sexuality filled the office, his retarded yet active sexuality. I rubbed my forehead, drank weak coffee, found it hard to breathe. He called the women in the office Miss Bethie, Miss Susan, Miss Isabel. He brought juice to the "ladies." Isabel called him the perfect woman's friend.

Late one night Leonard and I watched *Sayonara*. Again I sat on the sofa, while from the armchair he made mock-serious comments about "Red Buttons and I." The next day I was exhausted and disgusted. Suppliant women, I thought to myself. Supple, pliant, malleable, all those l's, low, before men.

He never asked about the man I lived with and would

marry soon, and I never mentioned him. We talked about my dog. Everyone knew (the women, that is, all the women knew) that this was part of Leonard's code. The women he fell in love with had to be attached, but the men they were attached to had to be shadowy.

I found myself trying to imagine his sexual fantasies. I suspected they were of two kinds: foreign and domestic. I saw him close his eyes and travel by bus through blond Germany or blonder Holland. His seatmate would be a girl of fifteen, alone and poor, heading to the city to keep an appointment. The nature of the appointment would vary, but her need for reassurance wouldn't. She would be wearing one of her mother's dresses: yellow polyester covered with Venetian canals, maroon acetate covered with swans.

In his domestic fantasy he would be living on a farm with his sister. They would drink lemonade on hot afternoons, welcome neighbours who dropped by, brush against each other in the hallway. At night he would lie in bed listening to her move around in her bedroom. Her bare feet would be small and smooth, her thin white nightgown just like the one worn by Shirley Jones in *Oklahoma*.

"I was thinking of you last night," he would say to me in the morning.

The perfect woman's friend. I came upon him once right after one of his headaches had lifted. He was at his desk, and it must have been around six in the evening because the office was empty. He looked spent. He looked like a man who had just made love. He reached for my hand and pulled me into his lap.

2

A year ago I was at my desk writing to old friends to tell them I had moved to Ottawa. I reached for my address book and it fell open to *Leonard Brooks*. His name coiled in black ink off the page. His address was less than a dozen blocks away.

I made myself walk down his street. It took several months to screw up my courage and even then my heart was pounding. A block short of his building, I chickened out and cut over to another street. Some weeks after that I made myself go all the way. This time I took in the stone façade, the old-fashioned windows with their many small panes, the recessed entranceway. I even looked up to the fifth floor and imagined him looking down at me. The building suited him. It was older than his apartment in Toronto, but he was older and so was I. Although it seemed to me that we had always been old, two little old people on little old canes.

At the corner there was a café not unlike one we had gone to in Toronto. From the outside it looked innocuous, white curtains hung in the window and rubber plants occupied the sill. Inside – I'm speaking of the Toronto café now – it was all chrome and leather, muscles and sleek hair. Leonard gave me his mock-alarm look and reached for my hand. "You won't leave me, will you?" The contrast between us and the others delighted him, and depressed me more than I can say.

We sat in rose-coloured light and he told me the story he had told me the day before. "Yes, you were telling me this yesterday." But he didn't stop. He had been waiting for the streetcar at College and Yonge on Sunday night. An elderly woman waited beside him, the only other person at the stop. They got on the streetcar together, they got off at the same place, they entered the same restaurant, and they ate their suppers alone. He was overwhelmed by the pity of it.

I knew what he wanted. The knowledge made me stubborn and cruel, full of an anger all the more powerful for not having been there a moment before. Even so, he was still my boss, and when he talked about the others in the office, when he said that Isabel and I were better than he was when he started, I looked up at him pained. Didn't he see that I was much better than Isabel?

Over dessert he went on about a party he had gone to the night before. He stressed what good talkers and interesting people his friends were, that he too had been pretty funny. I was too insecure and self-absorbed to understand the edge to his remarks. I felt the edge without understanding it. I felt hurt. I felt diminished in comparison, and compared deliberately, as I made conversation and he didn't listen.

The street was almost deserted. Toronto at ten on a Tuesday night. We walked to the corner and paused.

He said, "I don't know what I said over dinner, but something I said bothered you."

I shook my head. "The best thing you can do for me is not to pay attention to all of my moods."

He didn't walk me home. That was the aberration.

At my desk, ten feet from Leonard, I keep my eyes on my work. The office is bright. Several large windows look east and provide a home for long-legged and untended plants. An old office with old paint and old desks, a peaceful office when he isn't here. I type on soft green carbon paper and feel myself topple behind my skin.

How empty and sad to be in a B movie, playing the sort of mild blonde who appeals to mild men. I feel myself going – about to behave badly, bang the table, sulk, tumble apart as the pins holding me together pop.

The office is in the centre of town. From time to time Leonard still asks me to have dinner with him. At the end of the meal he always says, "I tip big," as he tips small.

This is the scene of our long, pathetic, unconsummated courtship which is variously a courtship and not a courtship in his mind, and variously a courtly friendship and a burden in mine.

3

"He was in love with you," Susan told me years later. We were in a restaurant with a wagon-wheel motif eating over-sized New York sandwiches, slowly.

"Maybe. Until he fell in love with someone else."

"No, I don't think so. I think he changed because you got married."

The wedding took place on a lawn under a tent and towards evening it began to rain. For a while Leonard sat beside me. He seemed wistful but not unhappy. He came late and didn't stay long.

At this stage, the summer of the wedding, I couldn't read him any more. He was still friendly, still attentive, but not as much as before. It was hard to measure, but I measured it somehow, sensed it. Later, when I pieced together his with-drawal, I found nothing overt, just a gradual diminution of attention, my sense of humiliation, and déjà vu.

I asked X about it. He had known Leonard longer than I had and one day I found myself talking about him. We were on Bloor Street walking towards Yonge. X was wearing sandals, summer pants, a white shirt open at the neck, and sleeves rolled up to his elbows. He always looked casually graceful to me. As usual my seriousness made him bemused and a little bored. I said, "You see, Leonard makes me feel so lonely."

"Explain."

At the corner of Yonge and Bloor he stopped to buy an ice cream bar from a street vendor. Only after buying it did he ask me with a look whether I wanted one. I shook my head.

"He's such shifting ground," I said. "His attentions are so hard to assess. Sometimes he's more attentive than other times. I mean it's always platonic, you know that, but his attentions fluctuate and that makes me less certain of myself and where I stand, and it makes me terribly lonely."

"I don't really understand that."

"Well, I'm being so inarticulate."

But of course my confusion was the message, and my need to be reassured that Leonard was the one who was screwed up.

"It's embarrassing talking this way. But I might as well."

"Of course."

"Lately he's drawn away from me. I think it's because I'm getting married."

"No. I noticed it before that."

"Then why?"

"It could be two things, no three. I have three hypotheses," and X smiled at me. "First, he doesn't like you as much any more. Second, you responded too warmly and that scared him away. Or third, he exchanged his crush on you for a crush on Susan."

The humiliation was complete.

So there was no defining moment as such. My friendship with Leonard turned over time, until finally all it was was something turning in my mind.

In the wagon-wheel restaurant Susan pushed her plate to one side, and I stared at the nearly untouched brisket, itching to eat it, but too, too what? The word timid hardly covers the territory. She fingered the collar of her shiny pink blouse, a practical successful woman whose self-sufficiency appals her friends – leaves us gasping at her feet like fish.

She said, "You don't really care about Leonard, do you?"

I looked away, over the heads of everyone in the restaurant to the corridor filled with shoppers. The restaurant was below ground in one of those huge office buildings on Fifth Avenue. It should have been in Calgary. What were wagon wheels doing in New York? She repeated her question. "You don't really care?" I was thinking about the half-life of old friendships, the residue. In my mind the friendship was still something, but out loud it was less than nothing.

"You have to understand that we were buddies," I said. But maybe we were buddies only in my mind.

Then I said something else, and my voice was so hard and angry that Susan smiled.

"I hate Leonard Brooks. I hate how he treated me. I hate how I behaved. I should have had more self-respect. You did."

"He was in love with you," Susan repeated.

I looked at her.

"I could tell by the way he talked about you."

I grabbed on to this. It mattered more than anything to me. Why should it matter so much?

Why should it matter? An odd sad competition, this one of who cared most and in what way. I've spent so long looking for an explanation that will show me in a better light and always I come to the same conclusion. I did Leonard's bidding as a friend and I do his bidding as a non-friend. What is it about me – this is the question – that draws his sort of attention?

My words were *I hate Leonard*. And Susan smiled.

"I've always thought of Leonard as a victim," she said. Which made me a victim's victim.

4

I leave the window and walk down to the Rideau River. It smells old. Runners go by, their feet on soft dirt. I find a bench out of the wind and watch sparrows peck the ground until someone shoves a leaflet into my hand. I look up, the man moves on. A religious tract with a picture of Billy Graham in a pulpit. Leonard loved Billy Graham, not the message so much as the power to move a crowd. That was Leonard's skill – manipulative innocence – playing now to an empty house. I wasn't the only one who got tired of him.

There was the time he wanted a western sandwich on brown and wanted someone to accompany him while he got it. He came up to me, put his arm around my shoulder and jerked me towards him. No, I said. He laid his head on my shoulder and looked up at me with dog-pleading eyes. I wanted to swat him. I said *no* and I pulled away.

He apologized later. Not in so many words. He came up to me in the afternoon and with a gentle smile talked about baseball and Bob Hope.

At a baseball game the smell of the lake blew over – between cigar smoke, peanut smell, Leonard's breath – caught by the wind and blown into my face.

5

I saw him again. Again I was in the library. I was coming out of the stacks and I spotted a woman I knew waiting at the librarian's desk. I paused to remember her name and saw Leonard standing to one side and in her company. My mouth open with the unsaid hello, I dodged behind a pillar.

Behind the pillar my thoughts took this form: You are the most cowardly shit on the face of the earth. Suppose they know you're here? Suppose someone else knows? You are a grown woman. How can you be such a coward?

Nevertheless, I stayed behind the pillar. I even pretended to read the announcements pinned to its surface. When I had collected myself sufficiently to face them – to go out and greet them both – they were gone.

A month went by and it was June. One evening on Wellington Street a friend and I got caught in a sudden thunderstorm: it pounded the sidewalk with such force that by the time we reached the library our pants and feet (my brown suede shoes) were black with water. In the lobby I looked up after lowering my umbrella and Leonard was five feet away: he was coming out of the cloakroom and he saw me the moment I saw him.

"Leonard."

"Now why did I think," said he, "that I might see you here?"

I smiled. He smiled. I kissed him on the cheek and he began to talk, a steady patter into my ear and not a word to my friend. In the auditorium I sat between them, knees spread slightly apart because so wet, shoes sopping, waiting for the author who came on stage and read, strangely enough, about Peter Rabbit's shoes. In the story a five-year-old girl sits under a lilac bush reading *Peter Rabbit*. She looks up and sees Peter, who asks her about his lost shoes. She just happens to have them in her hand. Peter and his shoes have come off the page.

We stood in the lobby, dripping wet, and compared our shoes. "And mine are suede," I said twice. But Leonard was too busy talking to listen. He remained talking all the way into the auditorium, up the aisle and into our seats. Talk, talk, talk into my ear so that I couldn't even turn to my friend (though once, in mid-Leonard sentence, I touched her arm and asked stupidly, "Are you still wet?") and so my friend was forced into silence by Leonard's talk and my complicitous listening. Out of courtesy, I was rude.

And always the question. How do we extricate ourselves? How do we get to the gate?

I looked down at his little black shoes – a small man, how small I'd forgotten – and his pant legs wet to the knee. He claimed not to have noticed how wet he was while my friend and I couldn't notice anything else, so wet were we. "And mine are suede," I said.

I had never seen us so clearly. Never seen so clearly his nervous insecurity, his self-centredness, his profound rudeness. Bachelor hustle yes. Spoiled yes. But not how he took me over. Monopolized me. Staked his claim.

Not just my passivity, but his active claiming.

Am I right to think it was nervousness that kept him speaking? His running chatter about a piano, his running anecdote about a concert, his well-shaped monologue which I chose to contradict. And right to think that my contradiction was responsible for his retreat?

We were in the garden, our feet soaking wet from the rain, hiding in flower pots and trying to escape. After the reading we moved out into the aisle. I moved ahead with my friend, Leonard fell back. I took care not to notice where he went and he vanished without a trace.

Never without a trace. Several more months went by and I attended a party for a friend who was moving away. I entered the living room and Leonard was standing there in his grey-green suit. He said, "Haven't I seen you somewhere before?" in a tentative-meaningful way that made me smile.

There he was, affectionate, intrusive, unsettling: the qualities that marked our friendship virtually from the beginning, and from which I withdrew over time and courteously, then over more time and less courteously, so that in the end it seemed to me that he was the one who withdrew and I was left to feel pained by the very outcome I had worked to create.

We sat side by side on the off-white sofa in the off-white living room with the fireplace blazing and various glass tables sending off reflections. A prosperous and successful setting for two people who always think of themselves as poor. It was easy to fall into the old shoe of each other's company. I asked him what movies he had been watching, then began to tell him about seeing *A Country Girl* when I was five, but he stopped me. "I remember you speaking about that," he said. "Clifford Odets, 1954."

"Ah yes. I was thinking Terence Rattigan."

"No. Terence Rattigan wrote *Separate Tables* and," he added with a heavy sigh, "*The Browning Version*."

I did what was expected of me. "*The Browning Version?*" I asked, my voice soft, interested, receptive. I coiled into his ear and for the next half hour he retold the story of Crocker-Harris, the failed schoolmaster about to retire early because of heart trouble. The joke among the students is that the Crock, who has no heart, has heart trouble. Only one student, Taplow, shows any compassion. On the last day of school Taplow brings him a gift, Browning's version of the *Agamemnon*. The Crock – who has learned only minutes before that the school has refused him a pension, and has known all along that his wife Millie is having an affair with Frank the science teacher – is so moved by the gift that he breaks down. He cries.

Until this moment Leonard has been telling the story in summary. He is seated in the corner of the sofa, his hands folded on his crossed knees, his small head slumped into his small shoulders, lost in the recollection of a movie and not unaware that he has the perfect audience in this not-so-young woman who has let him down. "You always had this effect on me," he will say later after retelling the story has reduced him to tears. "You always had this effect on me," in a tone of nostalgic reproach.

He catches his breath, stops speaking, then picks up again, this time with Millie's words when she learns that the gift is from Taplow.

"Let me see," she says. Then: "The artful little beast!"

"Why *artful*, Millie?"

Leonard gives the words Michael Redgrave's intonation. Redgrave is a good actor and Leonard is a good storyteller.

"Because, my dear, I came in this morning to find Taplow giving an imitation of you to Frank here. I don't blame him for trying a few shillings' worth of appeasement."

Leonard takes her speech very slowly for emphasis, and is undone. I watch him, but he doesn't look at me. He stares ahead, eyes blinking, mouth working a little, fingers laced together across his knee. I watch from my vantage point on his right, perched slightly forward on the sofa and turned towards him.

He recovers and continues, step by step through the movie, to the climax where the Crock gives a farewell speech in front of the school. He has prepared a speech but once on stage he loses its thread. Faced by a sea of students and teachers who despise him for being a failure, he finally says, "I am sorry for letting you down."

Last night I watched the movie. It was late and I was just as tired as I used to be in the days when Leonard and I worked those long hours together. How much, I wonder, is everything that goes wrong a factor of fatigue? Would we feel so many doubts and humiliations if we could just get a good night's sleep?

The movie ended at midnight. I took a sleeping pill, drank a cup of hot milk (lying back against two pillows with the hot white cup between my fingers) and went to sleep. In the morning it was raining. It had been dry for weeks and now it wasn't any more.

I woke thinking of the applause the Crock received for being an object of pity. He stood nakedly speechless, then humbly honest in front of everyone, and received louder and more sustained applause than the cricket hero who spoke before him. These dramatists. How they set us up. Next I'll be watching *Moulin Rouge*.

A few tears came to my eyes, for what they're worth. Some sympathy, for what it's worth. But in general I felt calm. Not exactly wise to Leonard, not exactly wise to myself, not exactly out of danger, but uninvolved and unalarmed.

It's still raining. Trees are in half-leaf, tulips wide open. Reality is a wonderful thing, it seems to me. Daylight, and Leonard in the flesh. He has come out of my side and is standing, now, on his own small feet. For a moment he removes his glasses and wipes his eyes with his fingertips. "You always had this effect on me," he says.

Is this what soothes me? His admission that I have had an effect? Because I feel soothed.

I sit close to him, our knees almost touch, in a room where we have more in common with each other than with anyone else. But I'm not drawn in. I feel him come out of my side and almost hear the tiny pop.

Little more than a stone's throw away, across the bridge and down a tree-lined street, he comes out onto his balcony. It has stopped raining and the air is sweet. I can't see him, but I know he's there. He can't see me, but he knows I'm here. He leans against the railing and then he raises his arms. His Loneliness raises his arms and blesses all those gathered below. After being blessed, they walk away.

This is the image I have in my head. I don't know whether it's my wishful thinking or Leonard's. I don't know whether it's cruel or kind.

A Clear Record

At Christmas I watched a beautiful woman use Nivea cream and a month later I bought some for myself. Ten years earlier I watched a friend fall in love and weeks later I was falling in love with the same man. Ten years before that I watched a dark-haired woman in Paris lean towards a man while she was eating salad, the soft pouches of skin below her eyes shining with some ointment that I assumed all Parisian women used. Now, on a day in February, I see the same effect in the mirror and realize the woman must have used Vaseline. I will continue to use Vaseline because women in Paris (I believe) used it when I was a girl.

Does it all come down to gullibility? Do things move forward in a line of cause and gullible effect?

I am in Paris, fifteen years old and faced with a slab of white butter which I confuse with cheese, unable to speak French and blushing deeply before my hosts. Easter break, daffodils in the Bois de Boulogne, wet shininess around the eyes of an elegant woman who is seated across from a man and manoeuvring enormous forkloads of salad into her mouth, a woman of middle age (I thought at the time) and of experience.

How do women get to be that way? In control and glistening with experience?

Bread torn rather than sliced, wine watered for children no matter how small, white butter like a certain skin-type: lard-like, carvable and thick.

Now here I am, years later, reconnecting through some sort of necessity with the woman in Paris. I cannot afford anything, these days, but Vaseline supplemented with Nivea. Even at $4.99 I wondered, turning the blue jar in my hands until persuaded by the memory of the beautiful woman at Christmas in whose bathroom I saw the same jar and from which I took a stealthy sample, applying it across my cheekbones and under my eyes, worrying about the telltale smell. At home, after my purchase, I am disconcerted by how heavily the cream lies on my face (like lard), until I remind myself that this was what the beautiful woman used.

Bakers use shortening on their hands. I know, having asked a young woman whose arms were dusted with flour. Crisco, she said.

That would be even cheaper, but without romance.

Perhaps my deep strain of gullibility comes from watching too many movies: from watching people fall in love on the screen and following suit in my mind. What could be safer? Then why did my friend emerge unscathed, while I continued to carry a torch for a man – X – who didn't appeal to me at all until I saw how much he appealed to my friend?

He has just called me. This is the first time he has called me in many years. He has called from Montreal, where he lives, to ask a favour for a friend who lives in Ottawa, where I live. His friend is dying. He'll be dead, the doctors say, in a matter of days. I listen to X in the dining room, seated next to the small telephone table. His voice is always the same no matter how much time has gone by, his light husky voice suggests that you have never left his thoughts. This is charm. I see the harm inside charm because of my old friend X. Listen to him go. He is telling me how he and his dying friend met, how long they have known each other, how many things they used to do together. He is telling me that his friend's wife believes their two small sons should speak at the funeral, not in person, he hastens to say, that would be too hard on them, but on tape. A family counsellor made this suggestion and so a few months ago the mother taped the boys talking about their daddy. The last time X saw her he asked what he could do and she said, Here's something you can do, you can edit this tape. And she put it into his hands. He took the tape home only to discover that it was unusable, the boys' voices were too far away and only the mother's questions were understandable.

Will you go to the boys' school? X is asking me. Will you go to their classrooms and interview them about their daddies? You'll have to interview several of the kids so you don't draw attention to the two boys. You'll have to get them to talk in such a way that your voice can be removed and their comments can stand on their own.

Our Christmas tree is up in the corner of the dining room. In three days we'll be leaving to spend Christmas in

Massachusetts. I tell him that. I tell him I'm willing to do this
for him, but not until early January. No, January is too late. It
has to be done now. I'm sorry, he says. I know it's a lot to ask.
I don't know who else to turn to.

He gives me the name and address of the school, he gives
me the names of the two boys, he says they are five and
seven. He says again that he's sorry, but his friend has only a
few days left.

He says, "I just want to serve the family."

I say, "You mean you want *me* to serve the family," but my
voice is tender, amused, friendly. For the first time his voice
becomes stiff. He says, "Well, his wife is counting on it."

About his voice there is always the presumption of intimacy,
as though he is speaking from the next room. Hi, it's me. A
huskiness I find appealing, and a subdued liveliness. From his
voice I know that he is pleased with himself for going to
such lengths for the sorrowing wife. But he isn't going to such
lengths. I am.

I drive across the city the next morning, thinking less of
the favour than the person asking the favour, thinking of the
phrase *you know I can never refuse you anything*, which indulgent
mothers say to their sons. I am a poor woman not being paid,
though he offered to pay for my taxi if I took a taxi, knowing I
wouldn't. I am driving, looking for the school, keeping track of
how much time all this takes, but good-humoured because,
after all, I have agreed to do this and therefore I am implicated.
I could have said, "This is a bizarre mistake. You would serve
your friends better if you told them so."

It is December 22nd, nine in the morning, and somewhere, I'm not sure where, although I have lived in this city for three years. There's the hospital, I recognize that, and now I recognize nothing at all, peering past windshield wipers and through snow for the name of the street. And here it is. Inside the school I wait for the principal. I have nothing to read, which is another big mistake.

The next day my husband will say, "He wouldn't have asked anyone he respected to do such a thing."

The day after that I say, "What do you mean by respect?"

My husband turns to look at me, we are driving south, he shifts his eyes back to the road.

"He thinks he can ask you to do anything and you'll do it. He thinks you're lucky to know him."

I stare out the window but Vermont is very grey and I close my eyes. I feel foolish and sad in the passenger seat while the kids sleep peacefully in the back seat and my husband drives and drives. He is thinking that I am never so soft with him, I never let him get away with this sort of murder. Who is this guy? And out loud he says, "Drop him."

My feeling of foolish sadness isn't new. I don't even mind it that much. But it does throw a light over everything. I have been in a small skit and now I am in the audience. The lighting is jerry-rigged for a church basement and I am the only one watching. X is nowhere to be seen.

The principal was a short, sensible, imaginative woman by the name of Muriel who sized up everyone she met within seconds. She sized up the woman on the fool's errand and let me know, kindly, that while everyone thought the children's mother magnificent they also thought her addled. The principal told several anecdotes about the lengths to which the mother had gone to make the daddy's death momentous, then said: children handle death far better than adults; during circle time one child might say, "My daddy died," and the next child will say, "And my fish died too!"

We both knew the mother's request was a mistake. What good would it do the boys to have their taped voices played at the funeral? No good at all. This gesture was for the mother, another way to milk emotion and garner sympathy. Or, to be more fair, it was the result of bad advice and confused thinking in the face of the tragedy she felt everybody was watching, when, in fact, everyone wanted to look the other way. Or perhaps that's exactly what she knew, and out of some instinctive aggressiveness she wouldn't let them look away.

Years ago I watched a young mother in a schoolyard talk compulsively to everyone about her baby's death. The baby had died only two weeks before, something accidental, I never learned what, but I watched the mother talk greedily to anyone who would listen. A young woman with a long dark ponytail and red lipstick.

The two boys came in to be interviewed one at a time, the five-year-old first. I told him that I was talking to children with special daddies, barely aware of the lie, determined not to leave empty-handed since I had come this far. We used the vice-principal's office. The small boy sat in a big green leather chair, I sat in a chair beside him holding the microphone, its head wrapped in soft black foam, and interrupting so that he would speak in sentences. He said who he was and who his father was, what they liked to do together and what they did at bedtime. After two minutes of this he said, "Can I go back to my room now?"

The second boy came in. He looked exactly like the first boy except that he was taller and wore a blue sweater instead of a red sweater. He also spoke into the microphone, saying who he was and who his father was. Then he said, "My daddy's sick. He's going to die, and I'm scared." And then he started to cry.

The principal was waiting for me. Sensible, perceptive Muriel looked at me and offered me a sweetmeat. That was the word she used, gesturing to the boxes of Christmas cookies on the counter. I ate two sweetmeats, then I went away with the image of the short, smart, soft-faced principal in my mind.

X's hair is grey now. When I last saw him five years ago, I teased him about it. He seemed surprised that I thought it grey but there wasn't a trace of any other colour. I teased him even more, but he didn't laugh. In fact I was harsh in a joking way as if to prove that he couldn't get to me any longer. But there was disquiet beneath my jokey toughness since, even in the moment of proving, I knew I was failing to prove by virtue of having to prove.

There is an expression and I'm trying to think of it, something about better judgement. He got the better of my judgement. Is that it?

I knew it at the time. Just as I knew the mother's request was a mistake. I was reminded of a wedding I had gone to once, the opposite side of the same coin, where the ceremony was equally prolonged and baroque, as if there were some insecure need to prove to everyone how much in love the couple was. It simply made me suspicious of the couple, then suspicious of myself. Perhaps I had never loved anyone so deeply. Certainly I have never had to face a husband's death.

I am always suspicious but never at the right time.

At home I phoned X and told him exactly what had happened. I told him that when the older boy began to cry I offered him a tissue and patted his shoulder, but I left the tape recorder running, and when he recovered I finished the interview. I told him the interview wasn't very good, but there was enough there to work with. I told him that on no account were we to do this to our children. I told him that I felt like a hack.

He laughed. He said he owed me a big one. I said I thought so too.

In January I went to Vancouver to give a reading and to my horror I began to cry partway through. I was very tired. At a certain moment an indrawn breath from a friend in the mighty audience of ten set me off, and I had to turn my back because I couldn't regain control. In my next life I will have Jackie Kennedy's tear ducts. But I will not have her breasts. No. I will have breasts like melons. On the flight home I read a book of stories by John Harris all the way through. I came to some lines that I read twice, and then a third time. "If you want any kind of work done you get reasonable people to do it. They will do a good job. They will remember to keep clear records and pry out the gold teeth before the corpses are burnt."

At a party two weeks later I learned from a friend that X had been in town for his friend's funeral. That's typical, I thought; he didn't even bother to let me know. Some weeks after that I received a letter from him. A note really, with a copy of the obituary. The obituary followed the usual declension in these matters from beloved to dear to loving, beloved husband, dear father, loving son. In his note X said he had called me, but I had been away in Vancouver. He said there had been standing room only at the funeral. He thanked me for my help – a lot to ask – so close to Christmas – so close to your trip – I didn't know what else to do. "See you," was the way he signed off.

I have to admire people who buy stationery of a certain size so they can write notes without writing much. The paper is undersized and they reduce the task even more by writing down the middle of the page as though descending a ladder, leaving huge margins on either side. It's a good trick.

I heard my husband say, *He thinks you're lucky to know him.* The note made me feel the same way.

Now, tonight, I wish for more presence of mind, so that I can deal with things calmly and out loud as they happen, instead of later and at length, silently, and without effect.

The Parents

Photographs were the most noticeable thing about the house. They covered the walls of the hallway and extended into the living room, past the piano, and into the dining room. It was a prim suburban house filled with sexually explicit pictures.

We had been invited for a simple cup of tea, but the table was set with deep blue china – plates, bowls, cups, saucers – and a white tablecloth. There was fruit salad, a large cake, and several varieties of bottled juice. Ted asked for a beer. Vern explained that he had none, would a cold drink do instead? Ted said yes, only for his uncle to say, "If you're having a beer I'll have one too," so that Vern had to apologize again, with Ivy chiming in – the two of them apologizing and offering, apologizing and offering – and Ted's Uncle Jerry turning everything down. "Forget it," he said. His rudeness flustered them even more.

Ted's aunt rose to get some milk. Ivy insisted on pouring the milk into a matching cream jug rather than directly into her cup. Ted's old aunt rolled her eyes. "I was just going to take my tea into the kitchen and add a drop of milk."

They were the sort of people, Vern and Ivy, who drove most people nuts.

"The poster," I asked, "the one in the hallway with the title about sexual dependency. What does it refer to?"

"It was a show," said Vern, "and a book." He put the book down beside me and Ivy whisked it away. "Not on the table," she scolded, "it might get spilled on." She put it on the china cabinet. After a while I picked it up and went over to an armchair beside the window.

Ivy followed me. She perched on the edge of the sofa, her knees pressed together and her hands very busy with each other. Seeing me turn to the introduction, she became even more agitated and came over to me. "I can tell you who some of the people are," she said, wanting to push me ahead to the pictures.

The first picture was called *The Parents*. It was a shot of Vern and Ivy seated in a restaurant, dressed up and stiff with anger. On the facing page were cardboard cutouts of the Duke and Duchess of Kent.

"Isn't that awful," she said over my shoulder. "Of course, he doesn't think of us that way at all."

The book was dedicated to the "real memory" of his sister. I skimmed several paragraphs in the introduction while Ivy talked over me – talked, that is, over her son – so that of several pages I read only one, yet I gleaned the outlines of the story. The sister hadn't "died" as Ivy had once told me, she had committed suicide by lying down in front of a commuter train when she was eighteen. Her brother had been eleven and very close to her.

I kept reading. In the week of mourning that followed he was seduced by an older man. I glanced back to make sure I had his age right, distracted by Ivy's agitated talk about Karen committing suicide – now she was using the word – and the effect this had had on Don: a fear of death, she was saying. I nodded and continued to read. He believed his sister had committed suicide because she was oppressed by sexual fear. Afterwards he went to a therapist who told him he might well suffer the same fate, and so he began to take pictures, obsessively recording his daily life the way it *really* was. His book was dedicated to the "real memory" of his sister, rather than the softened parental version of an eighteen-year-old who was terribly talented and played piano and died.

The piano was in the corner of the living room. No sooner had we arrived than Ivy pointed it out to me, "The piano our daughter played", her eyes greedy for sympathy.

All the pictures on the walls were safe ones, I could see that now. Unless you were told otherwise – Vern told me – you would never have known they were men dressed as women. "That's a man," he said to me of one particularly beautiful woman who was looking into a bathroom mirror. The shots were interiors of train stations, bars, hotel rooms.

"This is Berlin," said Ivy, "this is Tokyo, this is Paris," nervously, proudly, playing the docent in her own home.

The book, on the other hand, had pictures of a naked man masturbating, of Don's male lover weeping in *The Parents' Bed*, of Don beaten until nearly blinded by his lover. That was the one that drew from me an exclamation, and for a moment I closed the book.

"What is it?" asked Ivy, immediately at my shoulder, and I opened the book. "Oh – that!" and she turned the page.

"There's so much emotion in the photographs," I said. "Such nakedness."

"Yes," said Vern from across the room. "It's wonderful for art and just terrible for family life."

The juxtaposition of house and pictures haunted me that night. I saw the parents living their lives surrounded by a never-ending condemnation, wearing it like a scarlet letter in a desperate – valiant – attempt to own the son who felt disowned, to pay for past sins. And yet, like Hester, there was something theatrical about the wearing, something unintended by the forces out to punish. "I love the background in this one," Ivy said, "don't you?" She pointed to the yellow-green wall against which two young men had been photographed.

Honest and sly. Brave and calculated. Naked and posed. Each of these and all of them together, none of them cancelling out the other, even while the mother tried to cancel out her son's version of life and he tried to cancel out hers.

Ted's uncle had no patience with Ivy. He called her prissy and affected and ridiculed her attempts to trace her illustrious past. Done for show, on show, the Duke and Duchess of Kent. In the accompanying photograph, obviously taken against their will and after they had been forced to listen to things they didn't want to hear, Ivy and Vern stare grimly at the table. They refuse to look at their tormenting son. In the photograph of Don taken after the beating (he must have used a timer and tripod) his face is swollen – spread wide – and he is looking down too. All of them are desperate – the son desperately doing in the parents' pretensions, the parents desperately finding something pretentious about their son – and all of them noble because all of them in genuine pain.

We left them on the lawn. Only gradually were we able to extricate ourselves, sliding into the car and away, the windows rolled down to provide for waves and drawn-out goodbyes. (As hard to leave as it had been to enter; they kept us on the patio for the longest time.)

We drove away and they walked back up the front steps, through the screen door and into the hallway, past the poster about sexual dependency and into the living room, past the piano and into the dining room where they cleared away the blue dishes and dealt with the letdown after visitors, the curious emptiness of the house, the self-accusations about the lack of beer.

Ivy wouldn't let us go. She kept me in the hallway, holding my hand, holding my eyes with her gaze, her smile, her look of gratitude. She held my hand as though I were the daughter she had always wanted.

Before we left she offered us the remaining half of the thick chocolate cake, but she didn't want us to take it, we could see that.

I knew an Ivy and a Vern when I was a child. Ivy was an alcoholic, Vern was gay. They were mother and son and both of them played piano, living out their sorrows awash with drink and alive with mannerisms. My childhood Ivy was very beautiful. In a snapshot taken of her at seventeen, she was sitting on a stool, her pale small-boned face framed by lavish dark hair. Kim showed me the picture and told me the love story: her father had seen Ivy in an army canteen, had asked her if he could buy her a drink, and she had slapped him across the face. Kim said this approvingly and I took it the way she meant: This was romance. We were only seven.

Kim and I dressed up in her old taffeta gowns, long and full, patterned not so much with colour as with sheen. We pulled them out of a long closet near an old chest of drawers, maybe the very chest against which Ivy fell one night in a drunken stupor.

Ivy had big plans for herself and later she had big plans for her children. What became of the big plans were big emotions. She was big emotion in a small town. She wept over a stain in Kim's shorts, threw out shoes for having a single scuff, climbed into other men's laps. She practised a highly coloured sort of honesty. I use those words, reminded of descriptions of young women who died of consumption, their faces too rosy, too flushed: Ruby who sang in the Avonlea choir. There was something exotic, loose, sexual about such ill health; something exotic, loose, self-serving about Ivy's honesty. It was honesty as abandon, honesty as an excuse for saying anything and doing anything, honesty as scandal. She loved to press you with questions about how you *really* were, eager to hear confessions not for what they contained but for the way they bound you to her. Vern grew up and remained attached, his letters home were always addressed to Ivy.

One Saturday they invited me along for a drive in the country. We drove past a number of scrubby farms, down a hill and towards a sugar bush. Kim's dad pulled off the road next to the bush intending for us all to take a walk in the woods. Ivy was wearing a new white sweater not as a sweater is meant to be worn but draped over her shoulders. The first twig caught it and this was tragedy. She turned back, so we all turned back.

And what of the husbands who stand just to the side of their unbalanced wives? Calm, supportive, appealing in their quiet resignation, their honesty and humour. They are alcoholics too. Ivy cracked her head against the chest of drawers and died in hospital the next day. Her husband finished drinking himself to death a year later.

My childhood Ivy's hands were small and bitten, my second Ivy's arthritic, manicured, be-ringed. She held them in her lap, fingers sliding over swollen knuckles while she smiled, talked, documented our reactions. To live with the memory of your child lying down in front of a train, to live with your every effort to soften the memory repudiated by the second child, to live with no escape, and then to find an escape. Europe really appreciates him, she could say.

Vern seems to have absorbed the most pain because he makes no attempt to scatter it off himself – no attempt to hide it, deflect it, turn it into anything it isn't. He seems comfortable with his discomfort, not resigned, just aware it won't go away. Was his daughter similar, the one who quietly lay down in front of the train?

Before we drove away, Ivy said she would be taking her evening walk in the woods, and she did. It was six o'clock. She walked alone. A small breeze came up (I am imagining this) and she pulled at the sweater she had thrown over her shoulders, tugged it forward with both hands – a new white sweater. She walked slowly in low heels, nylons, skirt, looking down at the leaves. A small bag hung off her left shoulder. Once in the woods she stepped off the path and proficiently made herself vomit behind a bush.

There's a spot – a small clearing with a large flat rock – not far ahead. In a few minutes she is brushing the rock off with her handkerchief. She sits down and fishes in her bag. Vern will be puttering around the kitchen, making some-thing light for supper, a salad. I picture him washing each leaf, one at a time, and patting them dry between sections of paper towel. They'll have more of the chocolate cake.

It's rare to see anyone at this hour. Children are having their dinner, people walk their dogs later in the evening. Ivy stays alert though, and if she hears footsteps or voices she stands and makes her way along the path, taking her time, a housewife out on a stroll.

Away from the photographs she feels unburdened, her own childhood not so far away. She liked to hide things as a child, one of her mother's rings, for instance, which she couldn't find, then found and is wearing now, a small pearl ring which clicks against her wedding band. Her mother called her a clever squirrel.

She fishes inside her bag for the flask but her fingers stop on something else – a snapshot of her grandson holding a camera. A Pentax, and the grandson only eight. He loves to take pictures and he's so good at it, she'll say, justifying the incredible expense. She sent him the camera for his birthday.

I had forgotten the camera until now. The first time I met Ivy she pulled the snapshot out of her purse, dispelling one photographer with another and in a way so innocent, so unconscious, as to beggar description.

There's something else. Ivy did more than lead me over to the piano as soon as we walked into the house. She pointed to the youthful photograph on the piano top. "In this one," she said with a proud and quiet smile, "I'm pregnant with Karen." Pregnant – subtly pregnant – with the girl who played the piano and "died."

What I felt was a circling noose, a mother's circling noose, a self-congratulatory and pregnant mother making of something terrible a delicate and dishonest thing. Tending the shrine of a dead child and writing off everything in between, everything but the smooth and shiny piano and the smooth and shiny belly, the smooth and shiny secret since her belly wasn't noticeably pregnant (I had to be told). This is what is meant by loyalty to someone's memory. It's what gives loyalty, and memory, a bad name.

She entrusted me with this information. Held my hand before we left, looked into my eyes and willed me to see things her way. But here I am seeing things my way. Here I am trying to give disloyalty a good name.

The Reader

We were on a long ride home from the sea. Milt was
driving, Lorna was reading aloud, I was listening in the
back seat. We had set out early when it was cool and would
get home late the next night when it was still warm. It was
the end of summer. We stopped only a few times, once to
cool our feet in the ocean, more often to get gas, almost
never to eat: Lorna had made chicken and ham sandwiches
and she passed them around. We drove late into the night,
stopping at a motel where we shared a room, then on again
in the morning.

Looking over at Milt and back at me, Lorna asked if she
should keep on reading and we nodded. I think we both felt
flattered and touched that she would expose herself to us so
trustingly. I think we believed that she wouldn't have done it
with anyone else. It felt like a gift, this reading. The book
was one she had loved as a girl and still loved, she reread it

every summer without fail. It was a sentimental story about spunky imaginative Jane who reunites her estranged parents and finds paradise on Prince Edward Island. I listened. I knew the book. It had never been one of my favourites.

For two days Lorna poured cups of black coffee first from one thermos, then another. After dark she opened the glove compartment and poured by the small light inside, her small hands moving in the light of nonexistent gloves and reminding me of other things that remain only in name. We were a threesome, pleased with our friendship and gratified to be liked as the story unfolded and we made our way west. We drove along a highway bereft of trees, away from a summer house to which she was so attached that she allowed herself some tears.

The summer house was large and on a hill. It was everything they wanted their lives to be – gracious, open, relaxed and important, connected to the past and to every change in weather. It stood higher than anything else on the horizon and in its shelter they almost relaxed. They were profoundly shy, this couple. You went to their house for dinner, their enclosed and quiet city house, and they made you sit by yourself in the living room while they scurried about the kitchen. *No*, if you tried to enter or offered to help, go sit down, we'll be with you in five minutes. And you went back and sat in one of their high-backed chairs.

The house was old and beautiful. There were plants, there were fish in an aquarium, there was life – but none of it easy. You sensed what it cost them to have company, how hard they found everything, especially talking, and you felt for them and liked them for it. You wanted to help them relax, knowing they would be grateful forever if you did. They drank a lot. Sour red wines and Scotch.

My view of the road ahead was framed by the windshield of the old car and by their two sandy-coloured heads. Lorna's long braid wound around her head twice in an old-fashioned style that would have been motherly had Lorna been motherly. She was small, slender and pale. She dressed with great care. She avoided the sun. She almost never laughed. I remember her posture and wonder now if she took ballet as a child; we didn't talk very much about childhood. I knew that her parents had money, that she had gone to a sort of finishing school in France, that her mother often told her not to borrow trouble, an expression I had never heard before and liked. Milton's background was more rough-and-tumble, and his back was cement-like: head, neck, shoulders fixed by the grim determination so central to his character. He toiled in and through his anger which for all his plumpness was not the least bit innocuous.

Lorna's voice carried well. Occasionally she looked to make sure Milt wasn't grimacing, or asked if this was too much. He answered no, go on. He was in the mood to find her constancy charming, he had touched her hand when she wiped away her tears. She read about the ideal man – rustic, charming, artistic and kind – as different from Milt as can be imagined. Milt was short, crude and sour. He was ambitious and tense. He was quick to anger and long to hold a grudge. Yet he must have exerted considerable charm when he first met Lorna. His eyes, she said, were what attracted her. Those eyes.

It was easier to see what Milton saw in Lorna than what she saw in him. She was beautiful. She had an upper-class air reinforced but also softened by a sort of censorious neediness. She was always late and often flustered in a way that men like to indulge; yet she was quick to feel disdain for others. So was he. They shared a snobbishness that I disliked very much. But they liked and trusted me, and that goes a long way. They were very good to me.

They took turns, driving fast and well. Only once did I take the wheel and soon they took it back with smiles indulgent and patronizing. They were united by their forward push, relentless and driven, too rigid to be graceful yet seductive even so. I couldn't take my eyes off the passage of coffee from her small left hand to his tough and pudgy fingers.

A few months after our long drive home, Lorna phoned late and asked to come over: she had to talk. It would have been early December, there was snow on the ground and she was wearing a dark grey winter coat. She came in and tossed a newspaper on the table. Milt wanted things from her, she said, and not for the first time either.

I picked up the paper. It was folded open to a page of ads for garter belts and G-strings, black lace underwear and the most amazing brassieres. The ink on the page seemed heavy and smeared, the print was tiny. I put down the paper, went into the kitchen, and made tea.

Lorna was agitated and funny, more talkative in her distress than she had ever been or would be again. Her small white hands held mug after mug of tea.

The doorbell rang while she was in the bath. He stood in the doorway and his eyes – those eyes – were sick with worry. He was simple for a few minutes, sitting with me in the living room, saying that he would be lost without her. We heard her move around upstairs: footsteps, a door closing, the suggestion of clothing. I pictured black lace over skin that never saw the light, and light – small light fingers – buttoning things tight.

She came downstairs, her storybook hair unpinned and falling to Alice in Wonderland length. Milt went to her and kissed her forehead.

Lorna was remarkable for the care she lavished on her body, the lotions rubbed into face, neck, arms, elbows, legs, feet, the array of makeup carefully applied, the time all this took, and then the covering up. She buttoned her high collars tight and her long sleeves at the cuffs. She washed her extravagantly long hair every day – it came down to her bottom – only to wind it tightly around her head.

Everything had a lid. The bath salts were in a lovely wooden bowl and the bowl had a lid, the cottonballs were in a wooden box and the box had a lid, the tissues were in another wooden box and the Q-tips in another lidded bowl. She bathed every morning and every night, taking her time, making the bath last. After midnight she slipped on her old brown bathrobe and went down the hall to their bedroom where the furnishings were antiques, the curtains white lace, the dresser and bedside tables covered with doilies. Lorna would drop the robe to the floor, jump into bed, and pull the covers up to her chin.

Once, with the wistful sourness, the guarded openness, so typical of her, she told me that she and Milt might as well be ships passing in the hall at night. She said, if only he had a twinkle in his eye when he said it. If only, when he finished the paper at eleven and folded it and fixed her with his hard, impassive look, he had a twinkle in his eye when he said he was going up to bed.

Once she told me that whenever she left the house, even for an hour, she was terrified it wouldn't be there when she got back.

Those were troubled times for me. I had left my marriage, I was leaving my job, I was planning to go away. My doings seemed to entertain or at least distract her. She would arrive in mid-afternoon and stay an hour, talking so little that I talked too much. She offered me her loneliness and a certain gratitude (women used to visit each other this way, in the afternoons, with calling cards in their handbags). I bent to the task of cheering her up, proud of my ability to lighten her mood. It did us both good, I used to think: she needed a chum to balance her husband, I needed to be taken out of myself. It was work though. She was dispirited, heavy, and once or twice, insulting. Out of the blue she would twit me about something, my writing or my disorganized life, a small well-placed sneer that would surprise me.

Months went by and she did not mention her marriage. She never again referred to the ads, or, indeed, to Milt in a personal way. Apparently they had come to some accommodation. They had resumed their old pact or arrived at a new one.

I was part of the pact. I was the unthreatening confidante who provided the companionship that Milt failed to provide. Before me there had been someone else, a medical student called Debbie who had moved to Vancouver with her husband. Lorna had one close friend at a time. She chose you the way some men choose a wife. She set her cap for you. There was nothing oblique about her wooing. A dinner invitation, then steady phone calls, more invitations, an unvarying tone of sustained attention that would last, it seemed, for ever. I have to say that it was very nice. She called every day when I was sick, she checked on me whenever I was upset, she gave me gifts at Christmas, she remembered my birthday. I still have the complete Jane Austen she gave me and I still reread *Persuasion* because I love to follow the unfolding of Anne Elliot's second chance.

Lorna never had a best friend that Milt didn't approve. I suspect we were always of the same type: steady, serious, respectable, unalarmed. No high-strung failures, no boozy misfits, no giddy dames.

Then one day her tone changed. This happened about a month after I told her I was going away for the winter, and about two months before I left. I called her one morning at ten o'clock and her greeting was so brusque it took me aback. I spoke to her for a few minutes but everything I said made her impatient. This is new, I thought, she has never spoken to me like this before. She is speaking to me the way she speaks about everyone else. A few days later she told me that she had taken Susan to the symphony.

Where had she first taken me? The theatre. Stratford. Two plays in one day. She had driven their dark-blue Volvo and driven well, with the same hard determination I was seeing again as she swerved away from me and pursued a new direction.

A week before I left Toronto, Lorna and Susan gave me a going-away party. The party would have been Lorna's idea, an excuse to phone Susan frequently and a way to entrench their friendship. Many people came and I think everyone had a good time. I stayed late, talking to old friends beside the aquarium. The food was plentiful and good. After everyone had gone Milt and Lorna slipped under my arm a brown leather folder of satin-white writing paper. It was very kind, but I knew I was being eased out and it made me bitter.

I went to Mexico for several months. In the second week I wrote to Lorna on her writing paper, thanking her for the party and telling her about the widow I was staying with, the Spanish classes I was taking. Three months later I received a letter from her. I read it with pleasure, she said she thought about me all the time, but I did not write back. I came home in June. From the airport I took a cab to Susan's where I would stay for a few days until I found an apartment to rent for the summer. Susan opened the door and behind her stood pale Lorna. I shouldn't have been surprised, but I was. They embraced me in the hallway and we sat down, probably with a glass of wine, in the living room. Lorna took the green armchair to the right of the white fireplace. Susan sat on the grey sofa on the left. I sat in the other green armchair near the door. We talked a little about Mexico and a lot about Toronto. Most of what I said I addressed to Susan. Then, knowing exactly what I was doing, I scolded Susan affectionately for not writing to me more often. From her chair beside the fireplace Lorna said, "Did you get my letter?" Her face was puzzled and hurt.

"Oh yes," I said. "I did."

What were we really doing, Milt and I, on that long ride home when we encouraged her to read? The book was in her lap. She opened it. "Why don't you read out loud?" I said.

She looked at Milt. "You wouldn't mind?"

"No," he said, "I'd like to hear it."

The book was one of Lucy Maud Montgomery's, or as my daughter calls her, Lucy Mud. I put a pillow behind my head in the middle of the afternoon, but I didn't sleep. I asked for the book and read several chapters beyond the point where she had stopped. The motion of the car made me dizzy and sick, and I stopped reading after an hour.

We encouraged her to read even though we found the book ridiculous. We told ourselves she was endearing and congratulated ourselves on our tolerance. I suppose that's friendship of a sort. We were apparently so uncritical, and she so deep in her mood, that there was an air of trust between us. And perhaps, in that moment, the trust was real, and only afterwards did it come to seem false.

Last night I dreamt about them. Milt entered the dream first, his friendliness of the same old type – shy, arrogant, prickly, somewhat sexual. He spoke in the same old way, which was very little, but with a small smile to show that he thought you were one of the few people worth his while. I stood still in the middle of the kitchen floor. Milt moved around. He was as pleasant as he knew how to be, but without any easiness – a laboured, brooding man. Then Lorna came in. She barely acknowledged me. She offered a greeting, but one so cool – so calculatedly cool – so free of any desire for reconciliation – that it drove the words out of my mouth.

Now here was the surprise. She had a baby. In the dream not only were they still together, but they had a baby. She carried him against her chest.

Because they aren't together any more. Milt lives with a woman who bleaches her hair and wears striped nailpolish. Lorna has vanished from the lives of everyone who knew him.

In the dream he asked, "What happened to you and Lorna?" He asked the question and the air splintered – heat waves from a toaster – nothing major – nothing even all that painful. But how to explain that rapid and total deterioration, except to say that we must have expected and wanted it, Lorna as much as I. It had happened to us before and now we were exacting revenge for previous friendships gone wrong.

In September, before I left Toronto for good, Lorna and I got together. We sat in a basement café drinking Styrofoam cups of cinnamon tea. She drank her tea, then whittled down the cup until it resembled a crude lace collar. Those little fingers, which always buttoned her own collars so high, so tight, whittled down the cup until it didn't have a neck. We visited by rote. In the first moment, when I stepped into her office, a look of warmth rose on her face only to disappear in the face of something less from me. She turned her back and did several unnecessary things at another desk so that I would have to wait. Then we walked across the street to the café. She carried her satchel of work slung over both shoulders like a hump of misery, having taken up law, she said, because it was hard, and we found a table, one of those too-small tables, and sat down on hard white wrought-iron chairs.

She whittled away until nothing was left but the smell of cinnamon on her fingers. I asked about her clients, she answered briefly. I mentioned my travel plans, she made it clear they made no sense. I talked about a young lawyer who was doing extremely well, someone much younger than she was, and did my best to rub it in. And all the while that whittling, as though she were wringing my neck.

"I'm afraid the friendship is dying," she said of someone she had known since college, her oldest friend.

"The friendship is over," she said matter-of-factly, dryly, with a minimum of regret.

In Lucy Mud's book about Jane true friends seem to grow out of the ground like flowers, their loyalty and friendliness functions of the landscape. Lorna and I picked berries on the hills and near the shore, picked them into baskets and made jam in the kitchen. I remember how happy she was, how nearly relaxed. Three years later (a year after I last saw her) I wrote to her. I had been reading a book which caused me a moment of superficial and inconstant regret. In that moment I wrote to her. It wasn't much of a letter and she didn't write back.

The letter would have fallen through the mail slot onto the small carpet in the vestibule. Other pieces of mail would have spilled onto the floor, and seeing who the letter was from she probably picked it up last. She may have read it in the high-backed armchair next to the soft bubbling and peaceful lighting provided for the angel fish. She may have fingered her top button with little fingers, nails bitten to the quick. Her hair would have been wound around her head in the usual way, not a strand out of place. No wind would blow that house down.

I admired her for not writing back. She was flintier than I was, and I admired that. She was Churchill and I was Chamberlain. I admired her for seeing through me and for not giving me the easy resolution I was after. Sentimental people, I find, often have hides like steel, and she was my steely, sentimental reader.

Purge Me with Hyssop

Six weeks ago in early October, when golden sunlight and golden leaves were falling on a light covering of snow, I found a hummingbird's nest the size of a small egg fashioned from bluish-green lichen: a jewel attached by the hummingbird's spit to the slender branch of a beech tree. I touched the nest, wet from its smaller egg of snow, and marvelled at its shallowness. Hummingbird feathers are not feathers, my brother told me, but iridescent scales: a water-air fish-bird. Itself and not itself, and in the tiniest possible way.

The leaves, too, are and are not themselves. Green leaves are not green, they are green blocking gold. The green fades, the gold appears, it fades and platinum appears, the light tawniness of this dark-toned month. These various pigments are always there, inside the leaves. The temperature drops and the colour is released.

Today is November 23rd. I woke early and showered, then pulled back the curtain and stepped into cold air. Drying myself, I noticed a splotch of red the size of a nickel below my left nipple. I touched it. It was hot and smooth, and I was too disturbed to brush my hair.

The waiting room was full. I almost turned away. There were several children, several young people, and an old couple. The old woman was suffering from that peculiar depigmentation disease which her makeup did little to conceal. She wore a large amethyst ring and held a black patent leather purse in her beige lap. Her hands were lard-white and her neck mapped with white and brown patches where the pigments had gone awry. Her name was Leah and her slightly shorter husband was Melville. The nurse called their names.

I heard the name Leah and the old woman faded and a young woman appeared.

On my knees I go through old letters in a cardboard box. Dust, grit, old cheque stubs, old clippings, and only at the bottom what I'm looking for: a large manila envelope with *Leah's Letters* scrawled across the front. I am surprised by its size, can't believe all the letters inside are hers, but they are. In memory we wrote to each other for only a few years. The first year – our final year of high school and the year we met – there was no need to write. Then university, when I wrote to her more often than she wrote to me but she held up her end fairly well. Then the gradual decline until our letters arrived at intervals of years rather than months, and like splats on the windshield.

When I think of her now I see a splash of light, then particular facets glinting off glasses and teeth. A heavy radiance and a brilliance. She was on stage addressing the school, a beaming, fleshy, eloquent presence: a star pupil.

And when I think of myself? Not beaming, but broad in the beam; shedding so much that anyone could trace my route through school by following the long blond hairs I left behind.

We were seventeen and I was new to the town she had lived in all her life. We were side by side – a bus trip to some track meet somewhere – and she was plying me with questions out of what appeared to be genuine interest. *Plying with questions*. Those are words she would have used: she described my mother once not as a good sewer but an accomplished seamstress. It occurred to me, gratified though I was by her interest, that she couldn't be as popular as I had thought. There was room for me here, and I felt blessed.

That year was one of the happiest of my life. Overnight I became more capable. Exams were easier to write, teachers easier to talk to, students less intimidating. Leah and I directed a play together, and for the first time in my life I felt a surge of unshakeable confidence. The play was Thornton Wilder's one-acter about a small family in a car: I remember the mother seeing a dog on the side of the road and saying, "What that dog needs is a good plate of leavin's." It was a tender play and it occupied us for more than a month.

And now I hear my name. Bethie. Not the nurse calling, but Leah, and years ago. She saw me first and spoke my name before I recognized her. Her smile – that glorious smile that lit up a whole school – had changed to something slower and more tentative. Her hair was longer and touched with grey, her shoulders rounder. She had put on weight and she had never been thin. She took my black canvas shoulder bag to the car and we drove to her rented farmhouse in the country.

It was hot, mid-June, 1981. We were twenty-nine. Machines moved across the fields threshing hay, "Right on time," she said, looking away because she knew how many small animals were under the blades.

Her husband was in the kitchen. A large man, heavy-set, soft-spoken, defensive, kind. He rose from the table and left us alone, but by then – suppertime – our conversation had petered out.

I go over her letters at midday, the heat coming on, the light coming in, my heart sore – this is the word that comes to mind – for the loss of my friend. I think about the legendary student who resisted her reputation for brilliance even while she exhausted herself upholding it: chewed her fingers raw, strained her eyes until she couldn't see, wept when a missed bus meant a late assignment. Hour after hour she kept to the tightly drawn schedule in her small red notebook, and despised herself. She said she was more afraid of success than failure, and she was terrified of failure.

Christ must have been a relief. A great teacher and a generous marker.

She always felt I didn't understand. Which is true. I didn't understand and I resented her, not for discarding me exactly but for sidelining me while she went off to God. In the end she became a Baptist minister's wife.

I remember a few disloyalties. I can count them like beads. This is one, writing about her. The letter I sent when she got married is another. The times she left me behind for more desirable friends. The time she dismissed my future. We were in the dining room of her small house, we were still in high school, it was a sunny afternoon and she told me I would probably be a writer the way my mother was a painter: always trying but never great. I nodded because she was right, but I wished she hadn't said it and so did she. "I can't believe I said that," when I reminded her years later.

One aspect of the letters astonishes me. My handwriting now is almost identical to hers in the beginning, as though an hourglass has turned and one feminine figure has drained into the other. Is it possible that we have come closer together in this way if no other?

I understand her choice of husband now much better than I did before. How drawn she must have been to a man for whom academic excellence didn't matter. For various reasons he had done as poorly at school as she had done well, and no doubt they felt mutual relief at turning their backs on academic performance.

On the other hand, what did they talk about?

He said little over supper, ate quickly, rose from the table and went outside. Already she had admitted to me that she was unhappy, stricken by doubts about her marriage and about God, yet entrenched in both. She must have been so tired of my levelheaded questions, my unspoken disappointment, my unreliable fealty. She stopped talking about her life and didn't ask about mine.

I think she felt too much on view to see me as anything but an audience for her peculiarities. She was simultaneously on the surface of herself and hiding: so self-conscious that she was aware of every one of her words and gestures, and thought I must be similarly aware. She had been watched so long, viewed and noticed and remarked upon, picked out and set apart, that when she vanished there was no real place to go. "I have even more difficulty showing myself than in 1970," she wrote to me before my visit. "I'm sure you will be disappointed."

I was touched by that remark, yet angry. Who did she think I was? An examiner? Well, maybe so. Maybe she turned me into more of an examiner than I wanted to be.

I was aware – this is what hurt most – that she wanted and needed a different sort of friend, someone livelier and more entertaining, less intent and more openly fucked-up. I remember a walk over snowy fields when I joked about Peary and the Pole, but the joke went on too long and I didn't have another.

Being steady wasn't enough. It may have been enough when I was a child, but it wasn't any more. Besides, I wasn't steady. I looked out the car window at the fields of sweet-smelling hay and felt so accepting that I had no idea how demanding I was, how much I wanted her all to myself and on my terms.

I caught her in the act of brushing her teeth, bent over the kitchen sink with a mouth full of toothpaste. She looked up when I came through the door and laughed her merry, full-bellied laugh, her mouth frothy and white. That was the only genuine, unstrained moment between us.

And now the old urge to contact her again, as though with early affection you can wipe out late disaffection. I reread her letters the way I read the newspaper as a girl – for the sense of another life, a series of connections, a story out there. But this story is not awaiting me, it has gone by, and is still going by.

Newsprint doesn't have the same smell any more, but rooms, especially in November, have the same darkness. I used to sit on the old chesterfield in the late afternoon, the lamp on, the heat never turned high. There was a brown box radio across the room next to a large window, and beyond the window were fields undergoing the usual urban assault. From my bedroom upstairs I had a view of an abandoned farmhouse on a hill less than a quarter of a mile away. In the other direction, also less than a quarter of a mile away, lived Leah in a smaller, older house with her unstable father and her capable mother who was dying of cancer. Is that what has pulled her into such clear focus? Is that why I am at my desk reading her letters?

There's nothing the matter with me. A small infection, a course of antibiotics; the small nickel-leaf is already fading.

In one letter she is funny and rueful about her "sorrows," and after several pages of breast-beating about her obsession with good grades and her hatred of university, she underlines the sentence. *"You are the only one I can tell.* Anyone else I'm close to is not free. They believe that Christian students ought to strive to be good students, and my parents measure me by my marks, which heal all."

The last two pages are full of Bible readings. Her favourite passage for reflection is the story of David and Bathsheba, 1 Samuel 11 and 12. It goes with Psalm 51, which David wrote when Nathan the prophet came to him.

I take from the shelf the Gideon Bible I helped myself to many years ago in some hotel. 1 Samuel. Page 268. But Leah has made a mistake. It's 2 Samuel 11 and 12: David, unable to sleep and walking on the roof of the king's house, looks down and sees a woman washing herself. "And David sent messengers, and took her; and she came in unto him, and he lay with her."

I read the psalm. "Purge me with hyssop, and I shall be clean; wash me, and I shall be whiter than snow." The story strikes me as an odd one for Leah to be contemplating. The psalm leaves me cold.

In a music store I run my eyes over the cassettes and come to Leontyne Price. I hesitate, unable to choose between Price singing hymns and Price singing Mozart. Thinking of Leah, and out of nostalgia and a certain desire for atonement, I choose the hymns. At home I put on the cassette, but after five minutes I have to turn it off. An hour later I try again, drawn to the hymns and then, as they soar, repelled. All the old bitterness, the juices of rejection, fill my mouth.

In her last letter, sent after I wrote to say my marriage had ended and I was going away for a while, she said that at times she felt agonizingly trapped, but knew that if she ran away she would only have to come back. "God holds my life and I'll do what He wants."

When did her mother die? And what did I do? She died while we were still in university and I did nothing. I offered sympathy, but I didn't know how to talk to Leah about it, and I did nothing concrete. I remember her indirect words of advice. She had had to phone everyone, relatives, old family friends, colleagues, to tell them that her mother's cancer had come back. She was the only one who could make the calls because her father was already in the depression that would later require outside care, and her brother and sister were too young. Everyone, with one exception, reacted emotionally in a way that tore Leah apart. Only her mother's sister was matter-of-fact. "Well," she said, "we thought we had that licked, didn't we?"

Her mother gone, her father gone in another way, she turned to God. But that isn't it either. She had already turned to God, she was turning to God when I met her, although I didn't know it.

I went to visit her one summer in a small tourist town where she shared a cottage with other Christian students who went onto the beaches to save souls. They called it Rahab's House. Spies, I suppose, for Jesus. Anyone who lived in the house would be saved, and everyone else destroyed. "Only Rahab the harlot shall live, she and all that are with her in the house, because she hid messengers that we sent."

And then the slaughter of every man, woman, child, and animal. Then the burning. Rahab stayed in Joshua's camp while Jericho burned.

That Leah preferred the company of these holy-rollers to me: no matter how stupid the person, if they believed in Christ, their company was preferable to mine.

After she got married I wrote to her, scrawling on the envelope beside her new name, *Arrrgh!*, something I meant to be heartfelt and telling, even funny: a protest I couldn't restrain myself from making: Here you are abandoning yet another piece of yourself. But it was only fat-headed and offensive. After that she was even less forthcoming.

❖

Snow, at first a few flecks, and now many and larger. A real snowfall, driven sideways. Siberian dancers always portray snow with sideways gestures because snow never falls straight down. Leah would be interested in that, it's the sort of thing – not just the fact, but the museum where I learned it – that would have enchanted her in the old days.

Outside a woman walks by with an umbrella braced against the wind. And now the sun comes out and it's light again, having been, before the snowfall, so dark.

The weather takes me back to radio, the same intimacy and promise, the same nostalgia and loss. I don't work for radio any more and have shaky, mixed memories of when I did. I remember my mistakes. Yet the foundation is still there, just as it is with Leah: the old brown cabinet in the living room and the comfort it gave me; and dear Leah. I think these words, aware of their elaborate, untrustworthy sound, but the ones that come to mind nevertheless.

Thinking of the weather in friendship, I pull a book off the shelf by a poet of weather who retreated, like Leah, into privacy and religion. The poet writes about invisibility, italicizing the word to indicate the presence of the divine. The book I open was published in 1978 and the poems I like are at the beginning, the ones I can't stand, the overtly religious ones, are from the middle to the end.

Is it jealousy, I wonder, this feeling of rejection? Leah and the poet have something I don't have, a relationship, a friendship, which I turn, hard-faced, away from? Or is it just the pain of being left behind? (Leah leaving me for religion, just as my sister left my mother and for the very same Baptists.)

I phoned the poet once. Neither of us knew what to say. I had written to her to praise her poetry, she had written back, and now I was calling. I hung up thinking I had made a mistake. But it wasn't a mistake. I had something more now: the sound of her voice, her surprisingly smalltown Ontario accent, her discomfited way of speaking, her almost coarse manner, caught out by a caller and uncomfortable on the phone. Now, reading her poems, I picture a solitary woman accompanied by many things, a woman who knows the value of privacy and makes choices in its favour, as did Leah.

After this soft interlude of reading and weather, I see the final line of one of the later poems: ". . . the only unpretentious,

Jesus Christ, the Lord," and my rage comes back. Rage at seeing someone swallowed willingly and whole.

There were two resurrections: the one, when after six years of silence I asked around for her address and wrote to her, igniting the brief correspondence that resulted in the visit to her farm, then more silence. And the final time, when I was about to leave the country and wrote to her, and she almost didn't write back. The final letter I never answered.

Her invitation to the farm came in the form of a card with a picture of a lesser scaup on the front, a small pretty duck in flight. "I'm not entirely sure why the last two years have been so bad – a pervasive sense of failure, of hopelessness . . . if you come to visit I would take you to see the ducks. They're beautiful."

Leah parked the car beside the farmhouse and we walked through fields to the pond where she identified each duck in great detail, later giving me an article she had written about them. I kept the article for years, thinking it might tell me something about her, and deciding, finally, that it told me about the facts into which she had escaped.

Now I realize that the ducks were an escape into beauty, not fact. She turned with gratitude to the lives of animals, sick and tired of her own.

I feel ashamed and moved, only to come up hard against the final words. "Regards, L." There was a time when she signed her letters, *all my love*.

I find something else, a copy of a speech she gave at the end of school. I read it, then put it down as though my fingers have been burned. It's an essay about the importance of friendship as a source of stability in an unstable world. She uses the phrase "relationships with people" more than friendship, and all too typically I give the phrase a bitter twist. By then, I say to myself, she had already begun her relationship with One Person. Jesus.

Ashamed and moved because her despair is deeper than anything I've known. Because I underestimate her, am always underestimating people. Because I realize that the ducks were her great consolation and I wasn't interested in ducks. Because I wanted to be her consolation and didn't have a clue how to be. Because we had been very close and with some effort could have been still.

We had our unsuccessful visit beside the duck pond, and I don't think I wrote to Leah again until I was on the verge of leaving the country three years later. She wrote back, making it clear she hadn't wanted to write at all, her letter so bleak, so grudging, so final, so rigid. "I know my life is in God's hands."

She must have identified with Rahab: someone forced to be secretive because she knows something others don't know and is rewarded not for her knowledge – not, in the end, for knowledge – but for secrecy.

The doorbell rings. I turn away from the letters to open the door, and here is the woman from across the street in tears and a red sweater.

"My mommy died," the woman says.

I put my arms around her and invite her in, hand her several paper napkins and sit beside her on the sofa. Some years ago Ted got off the phone and said, "My daddy died," and I put my arms around him.

"I've been twelve years here," the woman says. "I've lost my grandfather, my grandmother, and now my mother. I wasn't there when any of them died."

There was a time when I would have befriended this woman and for a while we might have been close. Then the friendship would have become a chore – heavy, twisted, chewed up in my mind, chewed over with real and imagined slights, and with simple boredom. In my experience friendships have a natural way of going off, like milk left out of the fridge.

I don't know the woman well. The first time we met, I saw her desperate need for friendship and avoided her.

One Saturday afternoon in early spring Leah called: she was sewing and suggested I keep her company. I walked to her house (in three months we would be finished with high school) and for a while we talked in the small sewing room off the dining room. But our reticence was too evenly matched: she had too many things she didn't want to talk about, I knew myself too little and was too shy to say much. I questioned her instead and soon we fell silent. The material was light blue, a dress for the end-of-April dance.

The phone rang. Her boyfriend wanted to come over with his best friend. Leah grimaced and so did I: the best friend had taken me out a few times, but for several weeks he hadn't called. Soon they arrived. They sat awkwardly in the living room for a few minutes, fingering the copies of *Time* on the coffee table. Then they left. You're welcome to stay, said Leah, and I nodded – smiled – said goodbye to them. I sat for a minute in the empty living room. Then I got my coat and left.

I walked home. Halfway home they drove by – the four of them – and I lifted my hand and waved. They were four: the best friend had arrived with his new girlfriend.

Why would Leah cut her life to fit a friend's more solitary cloth? Not even I expected her to. But I was left behind in favour of other friends more than once, and my reaction (my mild acceptance, my underreaction) anticipated the overreaction (the brooding memories, the bitterness, the competitiveness in the seeming absence of any).

Of course I am the one remembering, so memory favours me. I'm almost sure she didn't call me that Saturday afternoon. I called her and she probably said, I'm sewing a dress, but you can come over if you like.

◈

From my bedroom window the view was black and white, glittering and cold: a white sky intercut by the rise of the hill, the slope of the farmhouse, the shaggy line of spruce trees. The house had been comfortable once and was beautiful still.

The way to the hill wasn't all that pretty. You walked off the end of the street into a rocky uneven field that opened up into a gravel pit. You skirted the pit, avoiding the silver needles of the hawthorn trees, and began the gradual climb to an old road that curved into the driveway and up to the house. Tin cans lay on the long porch, one step up and you were walking its grey boards. From here the school was below on the right and my house, separated from the school by fields, was on the left. In the fall I walked through golden-rod to school. In the winter, snow drifted against the stalks, bending them down.

Passage of seasons, friendships, towns. The farmhouse is gone now, the hill is covered with houses.

In that bedroom I listened to the crickets – sad, panicked, restful – and after a year I went away to university. We saw each other from time to time and wrote, saw each other more infrequently and stopped writing.

For three days I have been rewriting this story using a version I wrote several years ago. Only now do I look again at the last letter because I want the exact words Leah used, and something happens that has happened to me before. I am astonished to find the source of pain so graceful. Only a few weeks ago I came upon a rejection letter I received from a publisher several years ago, and found it so well-meaning and warm-hearted that I sat down on the floor and read it twice. All I had remembered was the no.

Leah wrote: "I hardly know where to start writing. I can't quite describe my emotions when I read that you had had a hard year, that you and Keith had separated. The truth is I probably would have put this letter off indefinitely, except

I have some kind of feeling that I want to contact you before you leave!"

The rest of the letter is much more interesting to me now than it was when I first read it. She makes the comment about her life being in God's hands, then goes into detail about puppetry, her new enthusiasm. I understand that I might have been looking for something more than puppet shows about Bible stories, but at the moment this seems a lot.

I reread some of the earlier letters, finding them so spirited and plucky and kind, so crowded with worry, turmoil and doubt, so laced with affection that, again, I think of tracking her down. I know who might have her address and I could find his address and ask for hers. But would it be any different? Or is it different enough now?

Her address in the final letter, written twelve years ago, is the one in Nova Scotia. It's hardly likely that she would still be there, though last summer I came close to finding out. We drove to the Maritimes and before we left I promised myself that we would go through her town, I would find a phone booth, I would look for her name in the phone book. But once we got to Nova Scotia, I could see that her town would take us too far out of our way, even though we could have driven there in less than an hour.

Makeup

I bought eye shadow for the first time when I was twenty-seven. I went into the Bay in Winnipeg and ran a gauntlet of glistening makeup counters. I stopped at the one that was least imposing and least expensive.

"Eye shadow," the young woman behind the counter said, "should match your clothes. What colours do you wear?"

I was wearing brown.

I said, "Oh, I don't know. Different colours. Blue," I said.

She produced an array of blues and I chose a luminous chalky turquoise and slunk out of the store.

At work my friend Sheila and I went into the women's washroom, amused and embarrassed, and she gave me a quick demonstration. For some weeks I applied the blue eye shadow and then I stopped. I stopped the eye shadow and I forgot how to apply it. In a few years I was a blank slate for the next friend.

Certain things I liked. The potent smells, the compact shapes, the bad poetry. Mauve platinum, spring mist, citrus coral. I saw them in other people's bathrooms – these circles and tubes – and they made me feel excited and foolish. They represented a world forbidden to me by my background. And what was that background? A family that ridiculed any form of display. I was, heart and soul, a Puritan.

Makeup reminded me of myself. Lipstick drew my attention to my lips not just in the application but afterwards. They felt different, matte, moist. And the smell, though slight, didn't disappear. I didn't want to keep noticing my lips all day long.

It reminded me of myself and yet I was applying someone else's face. It was a way of forgetting myself and of not being able to.

When I was thirty-one Lorna showed me how to do my whole face. We stood in her sewing room, two medium-sized women in front of a medium-sized mirror, and she did one side of my face and I did the other – an eye for an eye, a cheek for a cheek – in a foreshadowing of the end of our friendship. She gave me various things she didn't need – extra lipstick, powder, foundation – and these I kept and eventually gave to my daughter.

One winter when I was thirty-five and tired, Sophie came to visit. Once again there was a mirror and a friend instructing me in the art of makeup. She was laughing. She was beautiful, playful, and overly lighthearted. Soon she would be walking with a cane and using makeup ordered especially from Europe. Towards the end her skin acquired an unholy radiance, a sulphureous quality, a yellow-green luminous cast. Two weeks before she died, she bought a new pair of large silver earrings. Hours before she died, she was still insisting that a book she had lent be returned.

On this visit, however, she was laughing. She was amused by her choice of a husband. She called him "a man of commerce" and said her father finally approved. It would be her third marriage. There had been Rich, then Rickie, now Richard the man of commerce. His parents knew about the first marriage but not the second. Her friends were sworn to secrecy.

She stayed with us overnight and I couldn't sleep. At three in the morning I was playing with my lips and smelling saffron on my fingertips. Cool air came through the window after days of heat, but it was no help; its presence disturbed me as much as Sophie's. I shook Ted's shoulder.

"I can't sleep," I said. "I can't ever sleep when we have guests. I think angry thoughts. About my parents. About you."

"So every time someone stays over, you can't sleep because you're angry."

It's true. Why was I so angry?

Some countries are equally touchy about being invaded. Mexico, for instance, has been invaded so often it doesn't trust anybody. I jealously guard my borders having recaptured them from family and various schools. But what am I guarding? The contrast between the size of the fortifications and the paltriness inside eats away at me.

Ted told me that his first wife also hated guests. Is that so, I said.

"She was always pretending when they were around. She couldn't be herself and it made her bad-tempered."

My perceptive husband. His first wife also insisted that he heat her cup with hot water before pouring in coffee. Why, he asks from time to time, do I always fall for women who are fussy about their coffee?

Over breakfast Sophie talked about her wedding (she had slept well and on my pillow). She was sure there would be a wedding, but not sure when. The man of commerce had given her a single calla lily months ago, and promised they would get married when she received twelve. The number had stalled at eleven.

Then Ted told a story about a young woman in Mexico called Doris. One morning she met a man who in the afternoon sent her a dozen roses. The next day he sent her two dozen roses, the third day three dozen, and so on, until on the twelfth day twelve dozen roses arrived and she gave in: she agreed to marry him.

"In Mexico," said Ted, "men pile it on until the woman gives in, here they hold back."

The story so delighted me that I didn't bother to point out the price of flowers in Mexico, or to ask the obvious question. In their lavish generosity and excessive gestures, are Mexican men more loving? If I opened my doors to every friend for indefinite stretches of time and welcomed them without reservation or loss of sleep, would I be a better friend? Is my husband a better friend because he enjoys nothing more than sharing a house with untold numbers of people? Or is there something about such friendliness that flattens people – dispenses a uniform light – so that no one affects you and everyone is the same?

In this logic, which isn't new to me, I've chewed it over a hundred times, I become the true friend: the ugly duckling who turns into a swan. Cinderella sitting in the ashes of friendship.

Lying awake that night while Sophie slept, I kept seeing her hands and remembering the language school in Mexico where we met. In class she would eat sweet buns with small bites over the course of an hour all the while saying, "si, si, si," and laughing her musical feathery laugh. With her right hand she worked a soft ball of pink putty, and I asked her how much it hurt. She said it depended on the weather: When it was cold the fluids in her bones thickened, and it was much harder to move.

She was thirteen when her family left Tennessee for Chicago. That winter, on the way to school, her glasses froze to her face. At night she woke up with pain in her hands so intense that she had to soak them in hot water before she could fall back to sleep. In the morning her mother took her face in her hands and kissed it, then led her into the bathroom saying, "You need a little colour, my love."

Sophie was beautiful at thirteen and even more so when she got older. Her bones were her gift and her affliction. High cheekbones, a fine nose, a beautifully sculpted chin – and then hands, and soon feet, that resembled claws.

After she died, her sister called me. "She wanted you to have her makeup. Shall I send it to you?"

"It's strange, isn't it?"

"Yes."

"We used to put on makeup together. That's why." Then, "What would you do?"

"I'm wearing some now."

The makeup arrived in September. It was a disturbed, intemperate, exaggerated month. All the rain that hadn't fallen since June was falling now. My skin took to the moisture, and I was careless and liberal with the other moisture as we only are when something is free. First I read the names of the various petals, herbs and oils, then I applied the German lotions at night and in the morning, thrilled by the luxury.

In October the weather went dry and flushed, and I fell down the back porch steps. I lay on the ground for a few minutes, my hands pressed against my head, and when I took them away they were wet with blood. Two weeks later I fell down the steps from the second floor to the first, pulling my arm out of its socket. Now my neck had a leftward crick and my right arm was as weak as Sophie's. I went into my son's room. He was sleeping, and I marvelled at the purple cast of his eyelids, the ivory paleness of his cheeks, the fine redness of his lips – fascinated that an old lover's cool ivory skin was the skin of my sleeping boy. I drew up his blanket with my left hand.

This is such an old fear, the fear of being unrecognizable to yourself. And such an old desire, to make up, smooth over, have peace. I've said that I wrote to Lorna a year after we last saw each other. I've never written to Maureen and never will. Instead, I make up things that never happened, trying to regain control over a friendship whose reins I so lamentably gave away.

Maybe this is the truth: things don't get old and disappear, they remain in hiding and reappear. I look down at my son's face and see the colour of old anger and messed-up love, the movement of shadows under a stupid and forgivable past; I look at myself and see Sophie; look out the window and see summer fading and winter approaching and held between the two, squeezed till red in the face, the small body of fall. I put on rouge. It's called Rose Glaze and it must have cost Sophie a pretty penny. You apply it with a small retractable brush and it glistens slightly on your cheeks, like frost.

I can see the sort of writer I am, an emotional bag lady dragging along old friendships, old failings, old makeup and using them to keep myself warm in a shabby sort of way.

Sophie married her man of commerce dressed in an antique wedding dress, lacy and white, at a large and fancy wedding to which she invited all of her old friends, none of whom had anything in common with the new husband. Before the wedding she offered to give me all the Clinique cosmetics she no longer used, having switched to the European brand more suitable, she said with her wonderful laugh, for "mature" women. I didn't expect her to send the stuff, and she didn't. She was too busy with the last few years of her life. There were two miscarriages, the first caused by the medication she took for arthritis, the second

when she discovered she had cancer and needed chemo-
therapy.

She must have got as far as putting my name and address
on the box of old makeup, then stumbled across it towards
the end; and filled it with everything else.

Earrings

Late one afternoon about ten years ago, T leaned against the door of my office and looked at me. His eyes – his whole face – looked bruised. "I have to talk to you," he said, "somewhere private." We went down the hall to an unlit office where he sat on the desk, a dark slender figure wearing a light blue shirt and grey pants. I stepped between his spread-out knees and kissed him.

His wife had found one of my letters. He had been packing, she had come into their bedroom with my letter in her hand, she had said: You won't want to leave this behind.

He said to me, "I felt my heart go right out of me," and I saw him sinking down onto the edge of the bed away from the letter hovering in the hand of his suddenly underrated wife. He told me that he had moved out anyway, he was staying with his friends Roy and Joanne, but he needed time to think; maybe he hadn't given his wife a fair chance. Two weeks later he went back to her. Several months after that he left her again, but not for good.

One night, out late with my friend David and walking home, I led us off course by two blocks and rang T's bell. David didn't try to stop me. We stood on the sidewalk at one in the morning, a street without trees in a commercial section of town, and I rang the bell again. A bus went by. There was a streetlamp just beyond the door. T had moved to this building after leaving his wife a second time.

"Did he say to wait?" David asked.

But I wasn't listening. We went into the building, up a flight of stairs, and knocked on T's door. He opened the door. He had on a dark brown dressing gown and stood to one side when we entered.

This time it was less obvious to me that something was wrong. We spoke for a few minutes, then I went to the bathroom. On the way down the hall I noticed that the bedroom door was closed. I turned on the bathroom light and on the back of the toilet saw a pair of earrings, gold loops, side by side.

His wife was in the bedroom. She was lying on the bed watching the line of light under the door brighten as the bathroom light went on, and fade as the door closed. She heard the toilet flush, my footsteps, our voices. She heard the apartment door shut. She lay there waiting for him to come back.

For a long time the scene with the earrings was the one I remembered most vividly. Now the one in the darkened office comes forward in my mind: the almost Biblical darkness of a man found out by his wife.

After that the light changed. I came out of that dark office overexposed. A snapshot passed around.

Years later in New York, a friend and I went to a reading in a café downtown. The writer read a story she had written about a bush pilot whose plane crashed in a tropical forest. The pilot was not a mediocre man, she read, because he didn't have the quality that mediocre men share: he never had a sense of dislocation.

The sentence stayed with me as did the image of the wrecked plane being turned into earrings by the Indians who found it. I didn't understand the sentence, and after the reading I went up to the writer and asked, "What did you mean?"

"Well," she said, "I was thinking about the ability to possess a place with one's attention. The pilot was a man who, no matter where he was, was totally present."

That was the way the writer talked.

I nodded, and went back to join my friend and to think about all the mediocre men I had known and about myself as mediocre. I wondered if that was how the writer wanted us to feel. She wanted us to feel that we were mediocre and she was not. I knew the writer. She was Danny's new lover, and I had introduced them.

After the reading Danny kissed my cheek, affable and ingratiating as ever, his eyes searching the room for anyone important. He was always on the make, that man. Maureen wasn't there.

My friend and I ordered another cup of coffee. There was a reproduction on the wall of Picasso's *Jacqueline aux mains croisées, 1954*. Picasso was eighty in 1954. Jacqueline was his last, most beautiful wife. In the portrait her hair is a crown of thorns, her neck is grey and pillar-like, her left eye has produced a tear.

"Maybe luck in love should be redefined," I said to my friend. "It isn't just a matter of who falls in love with us but who dumps us. I've been lucky in the men who dumped me."

"You should write about that," she said.

And so I am.

A few friends vied with each other to be the most upset about the breakup of T's marriage. Isabel threw up in a public toilet. She took chicken soup to the suffering ones, and called more frequently. But most friends remained by us and fell away, intrigued but quickly bored by the sameness of his indecision and the sameness of my waiting. It was surprising that we were having an affair, but we were having the sort of affair you might expect.

One friend had known all along. T had confided in Susan who then spoke to me. She said, "Tell me a secret." And I told her.

She advised caution. "Stay away from each other," she said, "until you've sorted out your marriages."

We followed her advice for the most part. Once the letter became public she lost interest. She cut us loose to fend for ourselves, moved by superstition, I think, as much as boredom; she didn't want to be contaminated by our bad luck. I understood. I also believe that stories spill from one person to the next.

A few months after the reading Danny dropped the writer. Her name was Evelyn. I had met her while taking that film course I've already mentioned. I knew she was in a bad way, she had called several times, so I went to see her one Saturday afternoon. Her apartment was high and quiet with an excellent view of the harbour – her parents had money, they paid the rent – but Evelyn was a mess. I stepped into her physical presence: jeans, rumpled shirt, uncombed hair, tired face, coffee-to-go; and into her amusement. She was amused at the state she was in. She alternated between amusement and panic.

"I am training myself," she said, "just to enjoy Danny when I see him."

A few weeks later she called me to say she had just phoned Danny to tell him she wasn't going to phone him any more. She said, I thought you'd be glad to know this. It was late on a Sunday afternoon and already dark, I had been working when the phone rang. Evelyn talked at length about Danny and I listened. I even said his name from time to time, knowing that that was what she wanted to hear. I felt pity, curiosity, a certain horror at how familiar all this was, and then I felt resentment. Evelyn was using up my time. Ted came back from the park with the kids. Their faces were red, their hands icy. Annie leaned against me and I stroked her face. It was time for supper and she said so.

It's hard to have patience with friends who make the same weak mistakes you've made. I interrupted Evelyn to say that silence sends the strongest message and that stopped her in her tracks for a moment. I remember there were days when I swore I wouldn't call T. I would even congratulate myself for not picking up the phone, only to reach for it two minutes later. I would wait for his voice to soften when he heard who it was, and I would fill myself with the pleasure of this.

In the bathroom my eyes shifted from the earrings to the toothbrushes, the vanity bag, the pale green circle of birth control pills. The bathroom light illuminated the dark office of several months before: I realized how little he had told me and therefore how little he had told his wife. Seated on the desk, he had said, "I could have told her there were other letters. I wanted to say to her you should read the other letters . . ."

But he hadn't told her.

In the living room I said to David that we had to go. T followed us down the stairs to the lobby where he sent David outside to get a cab, his tone that of a man used to giving orders. But when he turned to me his voice was small and piteous. He said, "I am the unhappiest man alive."

I hit the wall with my hand and he jumped. I pounded it with my fist. He was thin and startled in his dressing gown, I was stupid and angry in my dress.

"I don't know," he kept saying when I asked him what was going on. "I don't know what I'm going to do, my life is so complicated, I'm so unhappy."

Then the rush of cold air. David had been quick.

That night I slept on David's sofa and in the morning we went for a long walk. The magnolias were in bloom, we touched several large blossoms and David said, "Why is it so exciting to see white after months and months of snow?"

T left his wife and went back, left again and went back, left a third time and appeared to be going back. I think I was better, but I don't expect anyone to agree with me.

Once I saw his wife in the street. She had a certain yeasty look that I would see again in Evelyn and Maureen – pale, left too much to her own devices, tired, nervous, over-full of dread and hope. She was wearing the earrings – same shape but much larger than wedding bands. She heard his dependence, overlooked the rest.

Oddly, or maybe not so oddly, Evelyn looked like Maureen. She was older and her skin was drier and more lined, but her colouring was the same and her features were similar. One afternoon she came for tea. She was wearing Guatemalan earrings and so was I. Mine came from a small stall in the market in Guatemala City, a glass cabinet full of old jewellery worn by women who may have died a natural death but very possibly not. Evelyn's earrings were a gift from Danny. She stroked them with her fingertips, then rubbed her lips which had small dry indentations made by her teeth. In the late afternoon light her hands had the dusty shininess of a pair of old kid gloves. She said, "I know Danny loved me. I'm sure he still does. He took me to the country, he bought me clothes, he gave me these earrings. So what was all that about?" Her tone was upbeat, even defiant, and the mixture of hope and hopelessness took my breath away.

How did he happen, that itinerant jeweller, to have earrings in such abundance? I wear mine while I sleep. Sometimes they snag on the pillowcase like persistent dreams.

Once I dreamt that T was coming out of a lake. He walked to shore in a swimsuit, then stretched out on the sand in some sort of mating position. That seemed to be the idea. As usual he wanted to make love and I, very attracted, said no.

We have all remarried. He and his wife, my husband and I. We all have children from these new marriages. None of us has seen each other in years, no contact. Just the odd thing I hear from Susan. I'm always reluctant to ask, afraid she'll think my curiosity a continuing attachment when it's only curiosity, I want to say, I'm curious about everyone I've met.

In one dream I saw him in the subway. He was on a lower platform, dressed in a trench coat. I went down to say hello, he turned and glanced at me, then resumed his conversation. It wasn't that he hadn't recognized me.

In another dream we crossed paths in an airport. I was going through a revolving door on my way to a bus, he was heading in the opposite direction. I felt my face light up. Instantly I regretted it. Again we didn't talk.

Another time I greeted a friend on her front steps and saw T in one of the wooden lawnchairs on the deep verandah. My friend put her arm around me saying, "You know someone here." She led me right past him to someone else. I woke up laughing.

In each of these dreams I walked to meet him with noticeable eagerness.

For a while the dreams, so much more forgiving than I am, interested me more than anything else. He always appeared in an attractive light, his wife never appeared at all. The dreams seemed to be saying that what happened didn't really matter, not the way I thought. Something had happened and the memory lived on at night, but there was a fluidity to it, a looseness, that suggested many other things might have also happened and might be understood in as many ways. The dreams turned all of these old wounds into a mild form of entertainment, and they continued for quite a while.

January through March

I dream about Cary Grant. We share a table in a restaurant and discuss where we'll next travel together. While we talk I write a letter in my head to Jill. A waitress walks past saying to another waitress, "Have you seen the bathroom?" I'm not sure whether she hasn't noticed him, or is so used to his presence that it doesn't interfere with her work. He is the Cary Grant of *Charade*, disconcertingly old and carefully lit. I never do see him all that well.

I wake with the happy, fulfilled feeling that I am entertaining him by being with him, and entertaining Jill by writing to her.

We used to watch his movies together. She would come in from Long Island for treatments at Columbia Presbyterian, then come to us for a few hours before going home. I set up pillows on the sofa and she lay back, weak and grateful. At the end of *North by Northwest* she sighed, "Too bad he was bi," and Maureen and Danny floated through the room.

Jill said she always knew which actors were gay. I said, "You *always* know?"

"Well," she said, "Laurence Olivier was a surprise."

"And Danny? Did you always know he was gay?"

"No. Just that something was wrong."

January, and snow falls like the flecks of light once popular in women's glasses. The sun is out, the street is wet. I walk downtown past the used bookseller's on Hawthorne and catch a glimpse of him in the window. *An Evening with Cary Grant*. I watched him again last night. The scene in the nightclub with Audrey and the oranges, when his look hooks into hers and they stop still. His face (the extra flesh, the widened softened features of age) comes into focus and the younger man – the young Cary – is suddenly visible. Desire brings his face into focus. Desire, interest in another, concentrates the mind. Audrey was wearing black, and Cary dark grey.

"Here you are," he said, opening the old-fashioned elevator door.

"Where?" asked Audrey.

"On the street where you live."

This question of where. I came home after being away for eight years and thought, I don't want to be anywhere but here, in this city where tall women go barefoot and strange children come knocking on the door to play, in this house with its cool evenings and long Martinis, long evenings and more Martinis, where people introduce themselves and bid you welcome. I walked from room to room, upstairs and downstairs, out through the back door and in through the front. I found my son on the verandah at seven in the morning with a bowl of Cheerios in his lap, staring out at the trees.

After dark I sat on the verandah and watched the moon rise and reminded myself to clip from the paper the times of its rising and setting. I went over phone calls in my mind. X's inflection barely changed when I identified myself, he could have been talking to anyone. Susan said it was hard to believe but she wouldn't have time to see me for a month. "However," she said, "I'm sure we'll get a chance to know each other." We had known each other for twelve years.

That's all right, I said to myself. It's not a crime not to be in demand. Don't let them know how you feel, don't be a burden and don't expect much. But I felt myself go small under the moon, and pained.

Isabel was tense, preoccupied, almost startled. "We can talk for two minutes," she said. "Where are you?"

And I told her.

The delicate and not so delicate fences went up, the veils of polite discourse designed to keep you at bay. But I had expected this. The return, the absence and the return, were significant to me but not to others; their lives had continued without me, while my life had stayed tied to theirs. I stopped making phone calls and wrote letters instead.

Outside the gladioli were dying. Inside the dahlias were sturdy in a vase. The house was perfect for keeping flowers – with each floor the temperature dropped five degrees and there were three floors; going downstairs was like approaching a cool riverbank. In this soft Canadian neighbourhood people stopped and spoke to us, but not for long. They came in for a beer but didn't overstay. They were civil and friendly. But there is always the hunger for more.

In November, I finally saw Susan. We had dinner together and I asked about old extinguished friends. I said, "You'll have to tell me the gossip about T and about Leonard."

"Not much gossip," she said. "T and Veronica are very happy. Leonard is Leonard."

I suppose the humiliation came from letting current friends see the failure of old friendships. There was humiliation, and a sense of failure, and an absence of pride, and it had to do with Susan's quick dismissal of my question and her way of not looking at me.

By December I was drinking Martinis straight from the freezer and thinking about the dilemma of being somewhere which turns into nowhere, and someone who turns into someone else. I met my name-alike just before Christmas. The other Beth – the new and younger Beth – was sitting on the floor of my old office at the CBC. Her hair was the same colour as mine, her face was not dissimilar. She was wearing the very sweater I had had on my back for three weeks. That night I shoved the sweater into the back of the closet. I told friends that I was changing my name to Ingrid Bergman. I began to watch Cary Grant movies repeatedly.

What do I find irresistible? The way he walks across a room, his size and stride, his face. The sense he conveys that he knows more than he says. The humour, the careful (couched) desire, and the impression he gives that his distance, this delicately balanced distance, will turn to love.

Pure affection can't begin to hold our interest the way ambivalence can. Ambivalence, ambiguity, so that we back away even as we approach. The gap between what we want to feel and the real feelings that lag behind – this doubt – is what he was so good at.

On the night of the eclipse I was doing the dishes, I was reading to my children, I was helping them into their pyjamas and brushing their teeth, I was tucking them in, and I was thinking: Susan never calls; she doesn't call, she never calls, she never will call. I was thinking that I had turned into Maureen.

My children's playmates had gone home and that was a relief. I had bundled them up and taken them outside to see the eclipse and to end their quarrel. They disappeared into the schoolyard and climbed the play structure (by day red, yellow and blue, but now black) and Ted came down the street.

I said to him, "I don't understand how we can be in the moon's way if we are seeing it."

The moon was high in the clear dark sky and we were on the sidewalk, side by side, looking up.

"How can it be us throwing our shadow on the moon if we can still see it?"

We watched for a long time. When we went inside Ted took a grapefruit, an orange and a lemon and explained that the grapefruit was the sun, the orange the earth, and the lemon the moon. "The earth goes around the sun," he demonstrated with the orange and the grapefruit. "The moon goes around the earth, and when they're lined up like this," he said, "like this," adjusting the fruit, "the earth is in the way of the sun's light shining on the moon."

But somehow the visual logic escaped me. I couldn't picture the earth blocking the moon. And then for a moment I did. I felt the sun on my back, mistaken sun and a raw memory from childhood. I was sitting halfway down the front steps, thinking how wonderfully hot the sun was, until I realized Dougie Lumley was peeing on my back. He was laughing his head off and shooting down arrows of pee. My mother was in the garden and didn't see.

I was the earth blocking the sun from my mother's view. I was the pissed and pissed-on earth.

The sun has become a large basket, the earth remains the orange, "but over here," Ted says, putting it far away from the basket, and the moon – he searches in the cupboard and removes one bean from a jar of black beans – "This is the moon. The moon is to the earth as the earth is to the sun."

I watch the black bean circle the orange and my thoughts spin endlessly around various friends, and it occurs to me that this is what I do all the time. The shadow I throw blocks my view of everyone I see.

Now I wait for three people to call – a friend, an acquaintance, and a woman I would rather not see again – convinced that the woman will call, the acquaintance will call, but the friend will not.

Is it the weather? The middle of January, the continuing rain, the lack of any true season. A need to befriend and be befriended, so that I call someone I vowed not to call, afflicted with a surge of forgiveness that makes weeks of resentment fall away. Is it a trick of the Martini to alter the landscape so slightly and yet so completely? To make me buckle under the need for love and not mind buckling? I sit in the canvas chair beside the phone and call Isabel but she isn't home. I call X and he is home but not especially welcoming. And so I have to waltz. I waltz over his mild surprise and indifference, and over my own disappointment, trying to appear entertaining and engaging and diverting and okay. I could say I called because I'm lonely and a little drunk. But I'm sure he doesn't want to know, or knows and chooses not to let on.

And so I shouldn't drink and I shouldn't call. People are busy (he was washing the dishes and didn't stop) and no more interested in me than I usually am in them.

How has it come to this? That on a Sunday night, while Ted bathes the kids, I sit downstairs and make phone calls to people I've written off?

And now it's Monday morning and I'm afraid that no amount of reassurance will ever be enough. I woke in the middle of the night convinced that my daughter had stopped growing.

Outside rain turns snow into a milky-blue platter holding the rain.

My kids are loyal to New York. They listen to *West Side Story* morning, noon and night.

"Tony fighted with the gang," says Mike.

"No," says Annie, "he never fighted."

"Just in the rumble?"

"Yeah. To help out his team."

Mike says, "Bernardo killed Riff, and Tony killed Bernardo, and Chino killed Tony." His eyes wide.

During the music he asks Annie, "Is this the rumble? Is it the rumble now? Is this before the rumble? Annie! Is this before the rumble?"

And during the rumble Annie will say, "Who's dead now? Who's dead?" And she will start to cry when we can't tell her. We don't know at what moment Bernardo is killed, and at what moment Riff. She cries with angry frustration that we can't give her the answer she wants, stirred up beyond all measuring by the music and the story, and sourly peevish at any snags in the flow of emotion.

The gunshot echoes through the house repeatedly (Annie covers her ears), the music forming a chaotic romantic punchy backdrop against which they play, eat, and fight so that the gunshot gets muffled and Tony dies and Maria tries to sing against the shouts of playmates who have come to visit.

Annie says, "Tony's already killed 'cause I heard the bullet."

Mike says, "Yeah, and the bullet went right in."

Annie says, "I like the beginning, the snapping, and 'New York,' and 'Officer Krupke.'"

"Officer Krupke is the cop."

"Yeah."

Mike says, "I like when Tony's killed, and the rumble."

"Why?"

"'Cause I like the bullet noise."

"But do you like what Chino did?"

"No. I just like the noise the gun made. Three people get killed in *West Side Story*. It's Tony, Bernardo, and Riff. Right? No one else got killed."

"I like 'Oh So Pretty.'"

"How about 'America'?"

"I do like 'America.'"

"Do the Jets and the Sharks have mothers and fathers?"

"Yes."

"Then they have to teach them not to do those things."

"Mike, let me tell you something. Riff has to live with Tony's mom because his mom doesn't want to have him. That's how bad she is."

Sometimes I think that if I could only smell the out-of-doors I would know where I am. If I could only pick up a whiff. And then, when it gets really cold, I do. On the very cold nights when the air crunches like the first apples of the season and things creak and squeal and are very still, then I smell the air. I smell it in the street and on anyone who comes inside, an almost sweet smell of frozen wool and fur and skin.

On such a night my little boy decides to go out and find the planets. Saturn, Neptune, Mercury, Mars. On the coldest night of the year, while I run a bath for him and his sister, he takes the celestial map he got at nursery school, puts on his boots and goes outside. I fill the bath and call them. Annie comes but not Mike. I go downstairs and search the rooms. A small noise draws me to the window. Mike is standing on the sidewalk without coat, hat, or mittens, looking up. It is the end of January.

On Valentine's Day snow falls as light and deep as goose down. I drop a shovel into the snow, then pull it out clean as a whistle; the sky pod has opened and poured out its soft guts. Inside the kids refuse to have a bath because it interrupts "Maria." I put the cassette into a portable tape recorder, set the tape recorder on the soap dish, and wash their backsides while the gunshot rings out for the ninety-second time. "DON'T YOU TOUCH HIM!"

Other presences are in the house: the roof stirs and moves with shifting snow. Under the heat of the sun it grows restless and sounds like someone turning in bed. Ants have begun to appear. There is a dead one on the living-room floor, and I didn't kill it.

Have the ants come to help? Come to sort through the bedlam of doubts, and in the name of love? They crawl along the bathroom walls past blond hairs hanging off towels and towards two faucets that drip. I think of curiosity taken too far, of love regained by a series of tasks, of help taking unpredictable forms.

A gift arrives. A beautiful coat of many muted colours my brother has worn several times but no longer needs. A fawn-coloured northern parka with a chocolate-brown outer shell and a grey fur collar. I take it out of its brown paper wrapping, and try it on, surprised by its lightness, only to be more surprised by something else. Every time I put it on, I go in the wrong direction.

I wear it when I walk to work in the evening. I walk up to Main Street, turning right into a hard wind and pressing on, lost in thought, rousing myself only to realize with astonishment that I am going the wrong way. Now I will have to walk fast under an underpass and along a curve of highway to make up for lost time. Cars pass me by – this figure in the handsome coat with a noose of fur around her neck – walking where people never walk. I arrive at work overwarm and surprised at myself the first time it happens, then surprised at the coat the second and third times. The coat has the power my brother had to tease and torment and comfort me.

Strong and continuing bonds are the ones that fascinate. What is this material that holds people together? What can we call it except loyalty of a certain kind?

I think of Maureen's house, the openness, the paintings on the wall, the pieces of fabric. I think of her stripped to the bone by husband and children, and wanting that, yet not. I see the road through the country – the one we walked – leaves falling away, branches going bare, the winnowing away of all feeling until I was finally unaffected by her.

For a time all my friendships took their shape from the one with Maureen, they were coats on that pair of shoulders. Would I have exploded at Carol had I spoken my mind with Maureen? Brooded so long about Leonard had I dispatched Maureen? Come to appreciate Jill without Maureen?

She continues to thread her way through my life the way a long absence does – something in the closet – an old coat you know thoroughly, a season that returns, a pattern that repeats itself.

It's March 20th and snow is still falling. Now there's a full moon and above the housetops, the edge of the sky is lightening – pearl, opal – the colour of certain buttons, opening, as the sky separates from the dark rooftops.

Several Losses

We were driving down 96th Street where it crosses through Central Park. A Sunday afternoon, about five, and a young woman was kicking the long grass beside the sidewalk.

Ted said, "She's lost something."

We were halfway down the next block and he asked, "What do you suppose it was? Did you see her beating the grass? She hasn't found it."

A moment later he said, "A key."

Her kicks were random, almost careless. It couldn't have been that important, either something easily replaced or of no great value and the search a matter of form. We drove one more block, turned right, passed a small park jammed with people, found two spaces on our block and took the second.

You don't often see people involved in the slow graceful act of unhurried looking, threshing the grass with one foot. I tried to find it, she would be able to say. I looked.

We had been visiting Jill and she was overtired long before we left. Her face had a papery quality, but soft, a tissue-paper curtain behind which her sickness continued. By the time we left even that fine paleness had disappeared, and she was haggard. A greyish-yellow fatigue had risen up from the bottom of her soul and tipped her head back against the sofa.

She had been losing things: a string of seed pearls, an earring, a necklace.

"It makes me feel nuts," she said. "It's not that I have to have these things, not that I couldn't live without them. But it makes me feel nuts."

"They'll turn up," I said.

"The pendant might. I might have left it at Maureen's. But the pearls are gone."

The pendant was a talisman she had worn for years. She had taken it off before a bath and misplaced it.

Her way of looking was different from the woman's in the park. She looked everywhere and not with the casual gestures of foot kicking grass, but desperately, incoherently, in places that made no sense.

"I keep looking inside the cups in the cupboard," she said. "I find myself shaking open books."

A month later we were in the grassy playground a few blocks from her house. The kids were on the monkey bars, her husband was with them. She and I stood off to one side. It was mild for December, occasionally the sun lit up her face. She had been sick for so long that her teeth were yellow and huge.

Before lunch and after we had been talking off and on, our conversation interrupted many times. Looking back I could see the thread of it clearly (I had picked at it with my questions, my fingers searching in the dark for something shiny), when there were any number of routes the conversation could have taken. The thread was her son Paul.

He had lost his job, his wife's eyes were getting worse, their new baby – a second child – cried most of the night. They had come to Jill's for Thanksgiving weekend, and it had been a lot of work, she said, but good until the end when it was "marred by their fighting."

She talked while making lunch and the conversation got that far. As far as her saying that Paul's frustration level was very low and she was very worried about him. It wasn't until we got to the playground that the rest of the story came out. It takes time for these things to be said and it probably takes a certain setting: not a kitchen, but a playground where you see small children against a great big sky.

Paul had hit his wife several times. After Thanksgiving she called "terribly upset" because he had hit her again.

"Last week I drove over there to talk to him, and she says it's been much better since then. But he says so little. I can't imagine being married to someone who can't say what's on his mind."

"What did you say?"

"I told him that whatever he does now will be with him for the rest of his life. The way he behaves now, the way he deals with Ellie and the children, is something that will stay with him for the rest of his life."

Her face took on a funny expression – puzzled, curious. She stepped close and said gently, "Why are you crying?"

The urge to punish. An image flashed through my mind and I was drawn almost irresistibly to it – an image of slapping my children across the head, over and over again, at some minor irritation. The pleasure of it.

The sight of my father kicking my brother upstairs, not restrained by the child's fear but impelled by it. By that small body at the end of his foot, which loosened and left puddles of urine across the floor.

The memory of Maureen kneeling beside a diorama – all children, all long patient explanation. It took me eight attempts to get her to finish the one sentence she addressed to me. Eight? Ten.

On what basis does friendship continue after the liking has stopped? Punishment. Friends punish each other.

Paul was twenty-two. He looked older and shorter than he was, already balding, his long torso supported by short legs. Each time I met him, I wasn't sure it was him. "Paul?" I would say, and he would nod and smile. Out of shyness, he assumed I wouldn't recognize him. That's what I reacted to, his assumption that he didn't register and the way he waited to have his assumption borne out.

I saw him again at the funeral. Nothing we discussed that afternoon in the playground – none of the several losses – anticipated the one that was to come.

Jill's husband died without warning after we moved to Ottawa. She phoned, and we drove overnight to the funeral.

Less a funeral than a gathering of friends. Jill sat on a chair in the living room, Paul's wife stood behind her with her hands on her shoulders, Paul stood beside his wife. Across the room, among several dozen guests, were Maureen and her mother seated on a love seat.

It was the moment before colour. April 2nd and there wasn't any green. Rather the softness of a female bird and that sort of colour: brown, lavender, russet. Fields were wet, streams were high, lakes were melting and yet the air was full of dust.

We had started out after supper and from the highway everything was visible – cows in their barns, women in their kitchens, children in their yards – because doors were open, curtains weren't drawn, and no foliage hid the view. We drove through dun-coloured landscape, through soft feathery pre-colour, to the grassy end of Long Island. In the morning I saw Maureen on the lawn.

We were in the car. The kids were asleep in the back, Ted was asleep beside me, I was sipping coffee behind the wheel and waiting for signs of life in the house. Out she came in a thin summer dress. She closed the side door without looking in our direction, and walked towards the back of the garden.

Through the windshield I watched her thin thin back, her shorter darker hair, her white hands resting on the brown fence. Then she knelt down on the grass, and even I could see that she was praying.

How easy it was to look at her. All pleasure is relief, William Burroughs said, and it was a relief to see her in the flesh and at a distance. She looked remarkably small. I was an adult returning to a childhood house. I was Gretel closing the oven door.

After a few minutes she stood up and turned around. I got out of the car with an extra sweater. She thanked me, and draped it over her shoulders.

We spoke a little. Danny was looking after the kids, he was going to take them to the zoo. "You remember how devoted he is. We don't think a funeral is the place for children. Unless, of course," and the old apologetic look crossed her face.

But it was all right. Everything was all right.

The funeral ended at two. Maureen and her mother helped Jill into bed: ninety-five pounds of bad luck, good grace and tears. Paul's childhood drawings were on the wall: a bicycle he had drawn when he was five, a praying mantis when he was seven, an interior of a room when he was nine. "He could have been a painter," she said. "Why do people complicate their lives so unnecessarily?"

Maureen left. She wanted to get back in time for mass. Yes, several times a week. The Catholic church in the old neighbourhood.

Her mother left with her. "Well," I said after they were gone, "I hope she likes bingo," and was gratified by the wry smile on Jill's face.

On the way home we took turns driving. When I wasn't driving, I was reading a book about people with strange absences in their heads. In one case a young man's memory was destroyed by a bullet, but his imagination remained virtually intact. Every morning he sat at his desk writing out his life story, searching through his ruined memory for words that eluded him by halves. He forgot what a dandelion was. "When it becomes faded, I remember what it is, but until then I just can't imagine."

People elude me by halves. I see only the good, then only the bad. I never see them whole. I have no explanation for this. No explanation for the coolness that stretches out between my periods of warmth, the disaffection between my periods of affection. I touch people when I talk to them. I put my hand on a newcomer's knee, or hand, or arm, and immediately the new person is drawn into an intimacy that I cannot sustain. People are charmed by my warmth and disconcerted to discover that it doesn't last.

My friendship is not reliable, but it reliably follows a pattern established in childhood of over-immersion followed by withdrawal, of infatuation (in its many forms) followed by aversion. I find the unlikeable in people. I become critical and harsh, and saddened that I am so ungenerous. Critical of them and of myself for being critical. And so self-disgust runs through my friendships. A profound disappointment in myself, even as I focus on the flaws of others.

The pattern leads here. To a woman past forty counting up friendships and arriving at small change.

Two days make a difference. On the way home there was a tinge of yellow around poplar and forsythia. Once again the air was one way, and what it surrounded something else. Not dry around wet, but colour around non-colour. Spring and winter tussled just beyond the twigs.

That summer Jill turned a deep aboriginal yellow and her cheekbones rose up in her face. She was a sick Indian queen. We knocked on her door and she led us past her wine-red sofa, through the blue kitchen and into her bedroom with its big, white bedstead as high as her cheekbones. She lay there all afternoon, getting up only once to make Paul a sandwich, spreading mayonnaise on his bread and swaying on her feet, stupid and stubborn with sickness and loss. The effort exhausted her. I put a pillow under her swollen ankles, her eyes kept closing, and then a storm blew in. It knocked the curtains about, rattled the pictures and turned the air yellow. We lowered the windows against the rain and watched the branches break. It must have been noisy, but I don't remember noise.

We remember the meaning of something when it leaves us. Or we lose something, and in losing it remember it as never before.

Jill – faded and beset by losses. When it becomes faded, but until then I just can't imagine.

2

It has been warm for two days, and now the snow is in an advanced state of rot. Friday was the warmest day all spring. Crocuses peppered the downhill slope below Laurier's statue, Colonel By held his rapier in the sunlight, Sir Somebody Head looked out at the ice-free Ottawa River.

Once I asked Jill how you make love last, and she laughed at me. We were walking down the road near her house, slowly because she was so ill. She said she felt as if a concrete block were inside her stomach, she could feel its edges rubbing against her. I asked my question and she laughed out loud. She said I was like her ninety-year-old aunt who settled herself into her doctor's office and demanded to know *exactly* how the immune system works.

And maybe that's the explanation. Love doesn't last – can't last – because we are so busy protecting ourselves from its loss. A pretty answer, and not very satisfying.

How can we maintain a steady regard towards people whose attentiveness ebbs and flows, and whose company we enjoy both more and less, and in whose company we some-times feel more and sometimes less? And yet how uncom-fortable the life – the loss – of this steady regard.

My brother's coat. I take it out and look at it, even though it's too warm to wear. The weather is too warm, indeed it's raining now, and the ground under the wheels of the car has turned to mud. This slightly-too-large coat. My brother two years older than I, and slightly larger.

The weather on his gull-island is probably the weather we have now. When he doesn't have a coat to send, he sends us weather.

3

The first hummingbird arrives and my mother walks down the path. We are at the cabin again: no leaves, red trilliums that smell like water, buds covered with velvet fur. We open up the cabin and it's full of winter cold and mouse droppings. We open the windows and sweep.

Light fills the whole woods. It shines on grey rock and on maroon petals held in the palm of green sepals. My mother's clothes are the soft green of something tarnished, her lips are trillium-red. Every morning she applies a layer of lipstick from a nearly spent tube to her upper lip, then presses upper lip against lower in one more act of economy.

We talk on the pathway. I tell her I've been writing about friendship and I use the phrase *the art of extrication*, saying how difficult it is to have companionship without being encroached upon: how easy to enter a friendship deeply and on someone else's terms, and how difficult to get out except crudely and with a lasting residue. Her eyes are interested and vulnerable. Our friendship began after I left home. A late-blooming companionship that depends on carefully orchestrated tact, love, distance.

Spring comes sooner in the old New York neighbourhood. We would be down to sweaters by now, walking on streets with trees and streets without. I remember one evening after an all-day rain, when the sidewalks were full of puddles which the kids loved. They touched everything they passed, running their hands over fences and the sides of cars. Maureen and I walked slowly, side by side, stopping to share the make-believe ice cream cones the kids bought in a vacant lot. What a pleasure her company was.

We walked over to the playground and even it was lovely, washed clean and nearly empty after the rain. A little girl with bare arms shared her candy with Annie and William – on the slide and then the swing, and later on the bars. I recognized the candy. Hard round tablets in pastel shades. She didn't say a word, communicating with her candies, her small smiles, her recurring presence.

On the way home the old man at the Korean fruit store gave Annie a short-stemmed discarded rose. She held it erect, fully aware of its beauty and significance. She looked so pleased, and she wasn't yet three. At home I put it in a little vase of water. She took the vase, drank some of the water, and carried it around from place to place.

In a room cooler than the rest of the house and with less light, I sit during a cold spring. A book keeps my coffee warm, gathering perspiration on its plastic underside: Elizabeth Bishop with a cigarette in her hand. The poems are about Brazil, although the one in my mind is *A Cold Spring*: the wilted crocus and something about branches.

So what have I learned? That on a morning in early May, I will be overcome by inner peacefulness, and it won't last.

There are forces at work – weather, distance, light – that gradually smooth tension away. And other forces – memory, thin skin, fatigue – that rejuvenate old grievances and bring new ones into play. That I have arrived at middle distance in middle age with not necessarily fewer friends or better friends, but with an overwhelming desire for peaceful friends. And that all of this is temporary, and yet always the same.

May 5th. And not a crocus, but a violet. And not branches, but hesitating trees.